THE
LEADERSHIP
SECRETS
OF
COLIN
POWELL

THE LEADERSHIP SECRETS OF COLIN POWELL

Oren Harari

McGRAW-HILL

New York   Chicago   San Francisco   Lisbon
London   Madrid   Mexico City   Milan   New Delhi
San Juan   Seoul   Singapore   Sydney   Toronto

Printed and bound by R.R. Donnelley.

McGraw-Hill books are available at special quantity discounts to use
as premiums and sales promotions, or for use in corporate training
programs. For more information, please write to the Director of
Special Sales, Professional Publishing, McGraw-Hill, Two Penn Plaza,
New York, NY 10121-2298. Or contact your local bookstore.

*This book is printed on recycled, acid-free paper containing
a minimum of 50% recycled, de-inked fiber.*

The Leadership Secrets of Colin Powell is not authorized,
endorsed by or affiliated with Colin Powell.

Contents

To my parents,
Rut and Herbert Harari

Acknowledgements

FIRST AND FOREMOST, I'd like to thank Colin Powell, the inspiration and role model for this book. As I will note in the Prologue, he had nothing to do with the writing of this book. However, the collegiality and support which we have shared over the last few years was instrumental in helping me tackle this project. I am grateful for the rich insights that I have been fortunate enough to gain from our relationship which began a few years ago, when I wrote what in the public's eye has become known as "The Colin Powell Leadership Primer."

Four individuals were really "there" for me as I plowed through the ups and down of the writing process, and I'd like to offer them my sincere gratitude. Dr. Gary Williams, the Dean of the School of Business at the University of San Francisco, where I currently teach, was always available with genuine encouragement. My father, Dr. Herbert Harari, read an early draft of this book and provided exceptionally valuable critiques of each chapter. Jeff Cruikshank, the head of the Cruikshank Company, did an exemplary job in helping to edit the first draft of the manuscript. Peter McCurdy, the head of production at McGraw-Hill, managed to do the impossible: turn a final manuscript into a finished product ready for mass delivery in less than two months!

I'd also like to thank my Fall 2001 Executive MBA class at the University of San Francisco for their useful insights on the Powell lessons that I shared with them.

Four additional individuals deserve special accolades and thanks:

I had a three month window to write this book, and I seriously doubt I could have done it without the help of my research assistant, Scott Brooks. Scott, a graduating MBA student at the University of San Francisco, did a terrific job in feeding me a steady stream of data and anecdotes which form the core of each chapter. I am in awe of what he was able to consistently do with quiet determination and ruthless effectiveness.

Jeffrey Krames, Vice President and editor-in-chief of McGraw-Hill's trade division, worked closely with me throughout the entire process. Jeffrey is one of the main reasons I chose McGraw-Hill as my publisher, and his intellectual prowess, editorial acumen, marketing savvy, and manic energy were such that I never regretted my decision. His input was not only critical in helping me during the writing phase, but also in expertly shepherding every element of this project to fruition.

My agent, Lynn Johnston, is someone I can't thank, or praise, enough. Yes, she did what a great agent is supposed to do during the early stages, but even more important, she remained an invaluable presence right to the end. She was always there for me, anytime, day and night, as a sounding board, an editorial critic, a coach, a strategist, a cheerleader, a marketer, and most important—a friend who really understood and believed in what I was trying to accomplish with this book.

My lovely wife Leslie has already received her share of accolades in some of my prior books, but in this case, she really outdid herself. During the three months in which I wrote this book, Leslie and I didn't spend a lot of time together. If I wasn't with clients, I was in my office hunched over a laptop surrounded by a mound of manuscripts. Leslie hung in there, took care of our home and family, helped edit some tough chapters, and provided me with a foundation of love and support that was essential for my ability to achieve my mission in such a short timeframe.

Again, to all the above colleagues, friends and family: thank you!

PROLOGUE

L ET ME BEGIN on a personal note. On September 10, 2001, I had worked long into the night making revisions to the book that you are now holding. So I was still asleep at 7 a.m., Pacific Standard Time, when a relative called and blurted out something about the World Trade Center in New York City having been attacked by terrorists. Still groggy, I flicked on the TV. From that moment on, I—like millions of other people in America and around the world—found myself glued to the images of that horrific tragedy.

Over the next few days, my deadline seemed unimportant. My *book* seemed unimportant. The project came to a standstill. Like much of the world, I was waiting to exhale—and I wasn't sure exactly how or when that would happen.

Finally, a colleague snapped me out of my malaise. She pointed out to me that the entire world context had shifted in a terrifying few hours on September 11. The rules had changed. If anything, a book about how Colin Powell approaches the challenge of leadership had become even more important to many people around the globe than it had been back when the project was conceived.

That advice got my engine turning over again. And one of the things that kept it going was the figure at the center of this book, whom I had come to know over the previous several years. Colin Powell quickly emerged as one of the key players in our country's effort to respond to the September tragedies and prevent their recurrence.

So I watched with more than ordinary interest as he conducted his numerous television briefings in the days immediately following the attack. Although he was at the epicenter of a new brand of war in a crisis situation, you wouldn't have known it to look at him. He appeared calm, assured, dignified, and prepared—just as he had appeared in numerous situations over the preceding several decades. Watching him field questions, I couldn't see any real change in his demeanor. The rules had changed, and dramatically, but—at least as far as the public could see—Powell had not.

In the weeks prior to September 11, Powell had been energetically criticized in certain media outlets. He was called the "odd man out" in the Bush administration because he stubbornly clung to a multilateralist approach in a cabinet that appeared to be dominated by unilateralists. Now, all that had changed as the U.S. reached out to build a coordinated global front against terrorism.

In the wake of the initial U.S. bombings of Afghanistan in early October, President Bush cited the work that Powell had done in helping to fashion an American response and build that worldwide coalition in the days following the attack. "The secretary and his team," Bush said, "did an extraordinary job of raising the levers of freedom to our side." And so, once again, Powell assumed a key leadership role in shaping the strategic path of the United States, as he had done in so many previous capacities.

For an author, there is some peril in being driven by the affairs of the present. We know that something momentous happened in September 2001, but because we're still *living* that experience—and may be for many years—we're unable to put it into any kind of meaningful perspective. So I had to resist recasting large portions of this book in the light of the terrorist attacks and their aftermath. That is a task for tomorrow's historians.

Nevertheless, as I put the finishing touches on this manuscript, it was clear that the emerging war on terrorism could provide compelling examples of how Powell's leadership tenets played out on a real field of battle. And so, where appropriate, I have drawn on these examples. For instance, some of the central ideas in one chapter were better explained by Powell's efforts at antiterrorist coalition building than by the examples I had originally included. Similarly, I have revised several sections to reflect the most recent manifestations of those principles. I hope that by so doing, I haven't overemphasized the history through which we are now living. Equally, I hope I haven't underemphasized it.

When all is said and done, this book is about Powell's leadership principles that have stood the test of time. While these principles are especially powerful in times of national crisis, I believe you will find them exceptionally relevant to your own personal and professional environment.

A BRIEF POWELL BIOGRAPHY

Colin Powell has had a truly extraordinary career. It's a child-of-immigrants' tale, reflecting strong values, hard work, discipline, exceptional standards, and high integrity. Today, Powell is viewed as a hero by Americans of all stripes—and also by non-Americans. But he is far from the conventional conception of a military hero. He does not wear his ego on his sleeve. He is not Douglas MacArthur, or even Dwight Eisenhower. Yes, he has achieved the kind of matinee-idol fame that makes it difficult for him to go out in public. But, as he made clear to me during a casual conversation, he's not particularly *happy* about that turn of events.

Because I will refer throughout this book to events from Powell's career, and not necessarily in chronological order, let me include a very short biographical sketch of my subject here. He was born on April 5, 1937, in Harlem, New York, to Luther and Maud Powell, both of whom had emigrated from Jamaica. Colin L. Powell grew up in the Bronx, New York, and in 1954 enrolled in the City College of New York, where he earned a B.S. in geology in 1958. While at City College, he joined the ROTC, where he became company commander of the Pershing Rifles and ultimately attained the rank of cadet colonel. Upon graduation, he received a commission as a second lieutenant and went on to basic training at Fort Benning, Georgia.

After basic training, Powell went to West Germany, where he served as a platoon leader in the Forty-Eighth Infantry. After three years, having fulfilled his ROTC obligation, Powell decided to make the Army his career. He married Alma Johnson in 1962, with whom he has three children, Mike, Linda, and Annemarie.

In 1962, Powell was sent to Vietnam, where he served as a military adviser. Wounded in his first tour of duty by a Vietcong booby trap, he received his first Purple Heart and was reassigned to the First ARVN Division Headquarters in Hue, where he worked as an assistant advisor on operations.

Powell found himself back in Fort Benning the next year as an instructor in the Infantry School. In 1966, he received his promotion to major, and in 1968, he returned to Vietnam, where he received his second Purple Heart (as well as a Soldier's Medal for heroism) for saving fellow soldiers from a burning helicopter. The following year he was back in the United States and was promoted again, this time to lieutenant colonel. In 1971, he earned an M.B.A. degree from George Washington University.

Powell's rise to prominence in Washington, D.C., began in 1972. He was selected as a White House Fellow in the Office of Management and Budget in the Nixon administration. There, he first encountered Director Caspar Weinberger and Deputy Director Frank Carlucci, both of whom were later instrumental in shaping his career.

In 1973, Powell was sent to South Korea as commander of the First Battalion, Thirty-Second Infantry. Among other things, he effectively dealt with serious morale and discipline problems growing out of drug abuse and racial tension. After a successful stint, he returned to the United States to the National War College and the Pentagon, where he made full colonel. In 1976, he was assigned to lead the Second Brigade of the 101st Airborne Division.

He then served in the Carter administration as senior military assistant to the deputy secretary of defense at the Pentagon, earning his promotion to brigadier general during that time. Continuing his ascent, in 1981 he was the assistant division commander for operations and training in the Fourth Infantry Division at Fort Carson, Colorado.

Today, Powell will tell you that he was always happiest when he was in the field, leading and serving in Army divisions. But his previous success in the halls of power—and his ability to dazzle the likes of Caspar Weinberger and Frank Carlucci—

almost guaranteed that he would return to Washington to play a role in the Reagan administration. From 1983 to 1986, Powell served as Weinberger's senior military assistant.

In mid-1986, upon being promoted to lieutenant general, Powell was sent to command the V Corps in Frankfurt, Germany. As before, commanding in the field gave him the greatest satisfaction, but once again, that role was short lived. Frank Carlucci, now Reagan's national security advisor, recruited Powell to return to Washington to serve as his deputy. When Carlucci was promoted to defense secretary in 1987 after Weinberger's retirement, Powell was named national security advisor.

In 1989, he received his fourth star, and was appointed by President George H. W. Bush to be chairman of the Joint Chiefs of Staff. Powell was the youngest officer and the first African American ever to be appointed to that position. Powell served as chairman of the Joint Chiefs from 1989 to 1993, under both Presidents Bush and Clinton.

In September of 1993, Powell retired from the military with full honors. During his career, he not only had personally commanded everything from small platoons to enormous units, but had also been a key player in leading American forces through wars, regional battles, and humanitarian efforts. He had been instrumental in shaping U.S. foreign and military policy for more than a decade. His star shone so brightly, in fact, that two presidential candidates (George Bush, Sr. and Ross Perot) mentioned his name as a potential future president during the presidential debates in 1992, and political operatives in both parties urged him to run for the U.S. presidency in 1996. Powell declined, citing (among other factors) family concerns about that particular path.

From 1993 to 2000, ostensibly his retirement years, Powell was one of the most sought-after public speakers in the world.

He also served on the boards of directors of Gulfstream Aerospace, AOL, and Howard University, and was the chairman of the nonprofit America's Promise foundation. This was a nonprofit that he himself had launched in order to help at-risk children build character, competence, and hope.

It would be unfair, even in a short biographical sketch of Powell, to omit a list of his honors and distinctions. His military awards have included the Defense Distinguished Service Medal, the Army Distinguished Service Medal, the Defense Superior Service Medal, the Bronze Star, multiple Purple Hearts, the Legion of Merit, the Soldiers Medal, and the Secretary's Award. Civilian awards have included two Presidential Medals of Freedom, the President's Citizens Medal, the Congressional Gold Medal, the Secretary of State's Distinguished Service Medal, and an honorary doctoral degree from Yeshiva University.

On December 16, 2000, Colin Powell was nominated by President George W. Bush to be secretary of state. After being unanimously confirmed in the U.S. Senate, he was sworn in as the sixty-fifth secretary of state on January 20, 2001.

WHY A COLIN POWELL "LEADERSHIP SECRETS" BOOK?

In his busy retirement years, Powell found the time to write his autobiography, and it's an excellent retrospective on his life, at least pre-1995. (I'll have more to say about *My American Journey* in a moment.) In addition, more than 20 books have been written about Powell. So why did the world need another one? What makes this one different?

First, and most important, this book is *not* a biography. This book is about *leadership*—the kind of practical, mission- and people-based leadership that Powell has practiced, and that throughout his career has translated into performance excellence and competitive success. My hope and belief is that whether you run a small family business, a large corporation, a National Guard unit, or your local Parent Teacher Association, you'll benefit from applying leadership the way Powell himself has applied it.

Let me describe briefly how Powell came to be the central focus of this book. As a professor and consultant, I've had the good fortune to work with a number of exceptional business leaders. Through that experience, I've been exposed to the qualities that constitute (and don't make for) effective leadership. In researching Powell and his philosophy, I became convinced that he espoused—and, far more difficult, *practiced*—many of the mental maps, decision-making habits, and other behaviors that characterize effective leadership. I want to share those characteristics with you, and that is why I wrote this book.

My personal experience with Colin Powell goes back to 1996, when I found myself on a speaking platform with him, in front of a thousand bankers at an IBM-sponsored conference. I suspect I was Powell's warm-up act, which was a good thing, because it gave me the opportunity to watch the former chairman of the Joint Chiefs of Staff at work, and to listen hard to what he had to say. He was witty, erudite, insightful, articulate, and self-deprecating. He was, in a word, impressive.

This strong performance prompted me to read his autobiography, *My American Journey*, mentioned earlier. The book not only was well written and a good read, but provided me with an unexpected professional payoff. As I read it, I started to take note of the principles and words that formed the basis of Powell's leadership philosophy. In fact, when I was finished, I was tempted to toss out just about every other leadership book in my library.

Over time, I boiled down these notes into eighteen little "Powell gems" and presented them as leadership principles in my monthly column in the December 1996 issue of *Management Review*. After each Powell principle, I wrote a paragraph or two giving my thoughts as to how that principle might be applied to a corporate venue. Because Powell had served as chairman of the Joint Chiefs, I titled the article "Quotations from Chairman Powell: A Leadership Primer"— a takeoff on *Quotations from Chairman Mao*. Since that time, it has become better known as *The Colin Powell Leadership Primer*. If you'd like to read it, the Primer is presented in the appendix of this book.

I sent a copy of that article to Powell as a courtesy. He told me that he enjoyed it, and he encouraged me to use it in my consulting and research. I was delighted to have established an ongoing relationship with Powell and pleased that he agreed to endorse one of my previous books. But to the extent that I thought about it at all, I thought that the Primer episode was over.

As it turned out, my prediction could not have been more wrong. In 1999, Powell phoned me and asked me, "Are you aware of the stir your article is causing?" Now, I had received periodic reprint requests for it (which I granted as a matter of course). But Powell was now telling me something altogether different. Apparently, my article was being reproduced like wildfire in government departments, on military bases, and in the offices of the many corporations that had invited him to address them.

Indeed, shortly after our conversation, the trickle of reprint requests I was receiving turned into a small flood. Every day seemed to bring fresh inquiries in my e-mail, many from blue chip companies and government organizations around the world. And that turned out to be only the tip of the iceberg. My research assistant turned up more than forty web sites that featured the Primer.

National publications such as *U.S. News & World Report* wrote about the Primer, citing one or two of the leadership secrets. *The Wall Street Journal* also covered it, in a page one story that appeared in March of 2001. Powell wrote me that at the beginning of his first NATO meeting as secretary of state, his European colleagues brought up the article. Colleagues sent me corporate PowerPoint presentations that took their text directly from the Primer. In a number of companies, the Primer became the basis for seminars and training sessions.

I began to get requests to expand the lessons in that Primer. Eventually, those requests combined to provide the spark for this book. *The Leadership Secrets of Colin Powell* is modeled after the Primer. In this work, though, instead of including a terse paragraph or two of commentary after each principle, I have now written an entire chapter on each. I have also tried to bring in complementary leadership practices and stories from the private sector, in an effort to clarify still further how Powell's philosophy can be embraced in a business setting.

So this is a leadership book, in a world that's already full of leadership books. But I think you'll find the material in this book to be richer and more application-oriented than that contained in many other leadership books. The reasons are twofold. First, of course, the book is based on the life and wisdom of Colin Powell, which is a very rich vein of experience indeed. And second, the commentaries I've included veer away from glittering generalities and apple-pie-and-motherhoodisms. Instead, I've tried to focus on the nuts-and-bolts, practical applications of real-life leadership.

WHAT THIS BOOK IS—AND ISN'T

At the outset, I want to make a few more specific comments regarding what this book is, and isn't.

1. **This book is not a biography.** To reiterate, this book is not about the life, times, and personality of Colin Powell. Instead, it's about leadership, using Powell as the source and role model for the principles, and attempting to apply those principles to any setting, whether it's corporate, government, or nonprofit.

2. **This book is not a book by Powell.** Since people have asked me about Powell's involvement with this manuscript, let me be clear: My relationship with Colin Powell is one that can be described as friendly and professional. Over the past few years, we have exchanged letters, documents, e-mails, and voicemails, primarily on the subject of leadership. Powell has wished me the best of luck in this book, but I want to emphasize that he had nothing to do with the writing of it.

   This book is authored solely by me, and I take full responsibility for its content. In preparing this book, I have drawn from a wide range of original and tertiary sources, such as personal communications from Powell, magazine articles, books, web sites, speeches, and other documents. I have combined that material with the research and consulting insights that I have drawn from twenty years of work with leaders around the world.

3. **It is not intended as a tribute to Colin Powell.** It should already be clear that I respect, admire, and like the man. But this work is no hagiography. Powell has his critics and detractors, and some of their opinions are included in the following chapters.

   Some of those critics say that he's been far too willing to use military force, and others fault him for being reluctant to use military force. Still others focus more on Powell as a leader and manager, asserting that he is not forceful enough, that he allows himself to be pushed to the sidelines by more aggressive rivals, and that he's more an "operations guy" than an innovator or visionary. He's been described by some critics as indecisive, too accommodating, overly cautious, and risk-averse.

This book is not the venue to attack or defend Powell. My intent in writing this book is to shed light on Powell's leadership style and to help my readers apply Powell's proven skills at leading organizations through complex situations.

4. **It is a book for a wide and diverse audience.** You don't have to hold the title of CEO, vice president, lieutenant-colonel, or even manager to find value in this book. Regardless of your rank or function, I think you'll find wisdom here that you'll be able to apply to your own situation and your own life.

5. **It contains several recurring themes.** In crafting the book, I wrote each chapter as a self-contained lesson, which means that any chapter can stand on its own. This means that the reader can tackle the chapters in order, or can simply choose to read any chapter individually. Each chapter offers its own unique learning point. At the same time, a few themes are repeated for emphasis, to ensure that the most important Powell messages emerge clearly.

6. **It is a "battle-tested" leadership book.** This book centers on the words and wisdom and philosophy of Colin Powell, but it does not end there. I have tested Powell's insights against the work of other experts and leaders who have conducted their own real-life research on the subject. I think that the result is a set of ideas that have been "battle-tested" and that grow out of systematic research as well as Powell's life experiences.

Let me end this prologue where I began it. Our world has changed—probably in ways that we can't begin to understand. One thing that's clear, though, is that our various enterprises, both public and private, will need strong and effective leaders going forward. They will need those leaders at all levels and in all functions. If you aspire to be one of those leaders, I hope this book will help you grow in that direction. If you already *are* one of those leaders, and are worrying about where your successors will come from, I hope this book will help you grow them.

Colin Powell has his own definition of leadership. As he puts it:

> **Leadership is the art of accomplishing
> more than the science of management
> says is possible.**

PART I

POWELL AS PROVOCATEUR

CHAPTER 1

KNOW WHEN TO PISS PEOPLE OFF

"Being responsible sometimes means pissing people off."

COLIN POWELL, the nation's former number-one soldier and current number-one statesman, is above all a *gentleman*. He's unfailingly polite—the very embodiment of civility. I would be surprised if he ever applauded the management styles of Darth Vader (*Star Wars*) or "Chainsaw" Al Dunlap (multiple corporate dismemberments). Simply put, Powell is not interested in intimidating people. Why? Because, as well as being a gentleman, he also is convinced that frightened people don't take initiative or responsibility, and that their organizations suffer as a result.

And yet this same Colin Powell is perfectly prepared to make people angry, even *really* angry, in pursuit of organizational excellence. His explanation for this seeming inconsistency is pithy: "Being responsible sometimes means pissing people off." Let's take a closer look at how Powell's personal comportment as a gentleman and a team player fits together with his sense of responsibility as a leader. At the same time, let's get a clearer sense of the organizational realities to which he is alluding when he talks about "pissing people off."

YOU CAN'T PLEASE EVERYONE

Effective leadership is exercised across a full spectrum of responsibilities, and also over time. Across an entire organization, involving a wide variety of people engaged in a multitude of tasks (both concurrently and in sequence), the leader must spark high performance and ensure the welfare of the group. Well, that's complicated. Even if the leader manages to get everybody happy with today's reality, somebody's very likely to get off the bus tomorrow. A leader simply cannot please everyone all the time.

> *Making people mad was part of being a leader. As I had learned long ago . . . an individual's hurt feelings run a distant second to the good of the service.*

Leadership can't be a popularity contest. Trying not to offend anyone, or trying to get everyone to like you, will set you on the road to mediocrity. Why? Because leaders who are afraid to make people angry are likely to waver and procrastinate when it comes time to make tough choices. Leaders who care more about being liked than about being *effective* are unlikely to confront the people who need confronting. They are unlikely to offer differential rewards based on performance. They won't challenge the status quo. And inevitably, by not challenging tradition, they hurt both their own credibility and their organization's performance.

Powell learned this lesson in his first leadership position: as company commander of the Pershing Rifles, his ROTC military society at City College of New York. All of CCNY's ROTC societies (like ROTC programs throughout the region) competed at a regional meet each year for various awards. Powell hoped that his Pershing Rifles would win both the regular and the trick drill competitions at the regional meet. As the meet approached, however, he began to hear discouraging comments about the student he had chosen to lead the trick drill routine. The student was distracted by girlfriend troubles, he was told, and had lost his edge.

Powell's problem was that he was friendly with this student, and so, although he talked to him about the negative feedback he was hearing, he decided not to relieve him of his leadership position. Predictably, the Pershing Rifles lost the trick drill competition—although they won the regular drill competition, under Powell's leadership—and Powell realized that his unwillingness to relieve his friend of command had cost the Pershing Rifles their second medal.

The issue is far deeper and more pervasive than a personnel problem. Organizations, like people, get into ruts. As the environment continuously changes around them—with new technologies, new demographics, new competitors, new consumer expectations, new waves of deregulation and globalization, and so on—organizations get *stale*. Systems, processes, and cultures become calcified. People get comfortable with what they know, and they fend off the unfamiliar. "Not invented here" (NIH) takes root, and the organization settles into a comfortable, backward-looking mindset. Nostalgia and rigidity get woven into the fabric of the organization.

This is a big problem, and it is one of the reasons why more than half of the companies that appeared on the 1980 *Fortune* 500 list no longer exist. They were big, dominant, and resource-rich—and they couldn't adapt. The fresh and compelling ideas came from their scrappier, faster-moving competitors. A few years ago, a vice president of a faltering *Fortune* 500 company told me ruefully that his company's financial swoon was due primarily to one factor: "We've got years of tradition, unmarred by progress." Carly Fiorina echoed this sentiment a year after taking the helm of HP in 1999, when she described the company's biggest challenge as a culture marked by "a gentle bureaucracy of entitlement and consensus."

This is the kind of environment that Colin Powell, gentlemanly as he is, is perfectly willing to disrupt for the greater good.

I'll be frank. From time to time,
I'm going to make you mad as hell.

CHANGE RUFFLES FEATHERS

Because Powell's career has been all about *change*, change is a central focus of this book. As we will see, changing things inevitably makes some people upset—even angry. But the fact is that external change is *endemic, proliferating*, and *accelerating*. In such a context, good leaders defy conventional wisdom. They constantly prod their people with "what if?" and "why not?" questions. They engender a climate of let's-try-it experimentation, demand innovative initiatives from people, and reward performance. And, yes, along the way they definitely piss some people off.

Think about the pace of change that has prevailed in the last decade or so. Before the mid-1990s, few people were using e-mail, and few were even aware of something called the "World Wide Web." People did business by phone, fax, and FedEx. Then that world got turned upside down. As a new reality set in, a certain percentage of people simply chose to dig in their heels. Here's Powell's comment on exactly this subject: the tendency of some people to fend off the new realities of a digital world by rejecting new technologies:

> **I'll bet you right now that there's no established organization where you won't find somebody who says . . . I know what I've been doing for the last fifteen years, and you're not going to screw me up.**

That's absolutely true. And the leader's role, in this situation, is to overcome institutional (and individual) inertia. Pissed-off people are the inevitable result of challenging the status quo. In fact, they may be the best indicator that the leader is on the right track.

THE PARADOX OF CONSENSUS

But at this point, there's another ingredient that I need to throw into the mix. Powell is a team player, and he would be the first to say that the leader's role is to generate organizational consensus. How does that fit together with a willingness to piss some people off?

The answer lies in Powell's particular definition of *consensus*, and how the leader should think about it. Emphatically, he does *not* equate consensus with "let's put it to a vote" or "let's chew on this until we can all get happy with it." That may be democracy, but Powell would see it as an abdication of responsibility. Instead, Powell follows his own formula for achieving, and then using, consensus.

To begin with, he is *crystal clear* about the general direction in which he wants to steer the organization. When he took over the State Department, for example, he communicated his vision in simple and compelling terms. He was determined, he said, to see the organization become open, collegial, and decentralized (that is, with field personnel making key decisions), fast, Web-centric, "boundaryless" (with groups and functions linked together, sharing ideas and resources), constructively confrontational (let the best ideas win), coherent in execution, and—most important—*performance-based* (no more rewards for cover-your-butt internal politicking).

After articulating these kinds of expectations, Powell was aggressively inclusive. Everyone was invited, and expected, to participate in the new game. Having communicated his "simple standards" (his words) in a speech to State Department personnel shortly after taking the helm, he declared, "*I want everybody to be part of it.*" That's both an invitation and an expectation.

But clarity of purpose and inclusiveness only go so far toward consensus building and organizational success. That's why no matter what the setting, Powell makes it his personal priority to *provide people with the necessary resources to successfully compete in the new game.* Two of his first pronouncements at State, for example, had to do with getting Internet connections for everyone and securing more training for foreign service officers. In his first major State Department address, he told his assembled legions, "*I am going to fight for you. I am going to do everything I can to make your job easier.*" It was a theme that he had sounded in almost the same words in several of his previous commands.

Concurrently, and in a related vein, Powell works very hard to earn a personal commitment from every member of his team. He is careful not to push too much harder than the emerging consensus will allow. "Everyone wants me to reorganize," he wrote me shortly after he took over at State, "but I'm not reorganizing until I've got these folks on my side and believing in my leadership."

So Powell is very deliberate and methodical as he sets out to spark change in his organization. Even as he lays out his new agenda and starts the change ball rolling, he spends an enormous amount of time listening, learning, and involving people in the change process. He does this to make himself smarter—a theme to which we'll return in later chapters. But he also does it to enhance his employees' understanding of the whys and hows of change, to get their input and participation, to boost morale, and to build trust. And all of this creates the necessary foundation for even more ambitious changes in the future. Powell's point is that change is not a one-shot deal. It's a continuous, dynamic process that people must understand and accept. The leader's job is to build a direction and *foundation* for sustained change.

But don't assume that Powell is prepared to wait patiently until everybody gets into line and declares himself or herself to be ready for change. Let's face it: There are some people who will *never* come around. And there are some circumstances that are too dire or desperate to allow for *any* sort of gradual process. In such cases, as we shall see in subsequent chapters, Powell is perfectly willing to throw himself out in front of the pack.

As a top-ranking military officer, for example, he was willing to take the lead and publicly embrace policies designed to shake up and recast the U.S. military at the end of the Cold War. It's hard to imagine a public stance that would be more likely to piss off a lot of people with vested interests in the old way of doing things—including a lot of the people under his command.

So seek consensus, but be prepared to move ahead decisively (and risk pissing people off) when the organization demands it. "There are times when leaders have to act," says Powell's colleague in the Bush cabinet, Secretary of Defense Donald Rumsfeld, "[even] when the public's not there yet."

> *I only have to do so much compromising.*
> *There comes a time when I can*
> *just say, 'Do it!'*

Bottom line: even as Powell expects to upset people with his performance and change agendas, he works hard to build consensus for those very agendas. Good leaders are comfortable with that paradox.

WHO *NOT* TO PISS OFF

There is one more significant corollary to "Pissing People Off the Powell Way" that needs to be taken into account. And that is, *a good leader ensures that the right people are getting pissed off, and the wrong people aren't.* Phrasing it a little more positively, Powell believes that *good leaders focus ceaselessly on making sure that their best people are the most satisfied.*

At every opportunity, Powell reiterates his belief that, ultimately, it is *people*—not plans, systems, structures, or budgets—who make the difference between organizational success and organizational failure. Good people develop the best ideas. They generate the most creative action plans. They implement those plans better than anybody else.

Well, you don't attract, retain, and inspire these remarkable people by treating everyone the same. You have to *differentiate*. This means not only rewarding top performers, but also refusing to coddle the also-rans. On at least one occasion,

Powell the commanding officer got into trouble for being slow to award medals and honors to large numbers of his troops. Yes, many of these individuals had *performed*, but, as Powell saw it, they hadn't *excelled*. Medals, Powell felt, should not be standard issue, as he believed they had become during the Vietnam War. Ribbons, stars, and commendations ought to be reserved for the overachievers.

Inflation debases currencies and medals.

Your best people are those who support your agenda and who deliver the goods. Those people expect more and deserve more, whether those rewards take the form of additional compensation, accolades, career advancement, assignments to plum projects, or personal development opportunities. If they don't get what they expect and deserve, they become deflated, demotivated, and cynical. Because they're marketable, they're the first ones to update their résumés when they're unhappy. And for organizations competing in today's knowledge economy, that can be a recipe for disaster.

This is not a zero-sum situation, of course. In the unlikely event that everyone in the organization is making a significant commitment and contribution to the agenda, then everyone should receive significant rewards. But in most cases, simply awarding across-the-board increases, percentage bonuses, or the like is just a leadership cop-out. Even this early in his tenure at State, Powell has already drilled home the message that performance counts. And if that's true, then high performers need to be properly rewarded, and underachievers need to be reviewed, retooled, or removed.

What if lower performers don't retool satisfactorily and, despite the leader's efforts to help them improve their performance, wind up dissatisfied with their lower rewards? Well, so be it. Pissing off these kinds of people can be good for the organization. If they leave, the organization is likely to benefit. If they *don't* leave, the good people eventually will, and the organization will suffer. Powell, despite his gentlemanly ways, is quite willing to turn the heat up under low performers.

> *If you perform well, we'll get along fine.*
> *If you don't, you are going to*
> *give me push-ups.*

In the military battlefield, the leader's distinction between good and subpar performance can easily mean the difference between victory and defeat, which is perhaps why Powell is so uncompromising in his stance. Savvy private-sector leaders understand that this distinction can mean the difference between corporate victory and defeat.

That is why successful CEOs like GE's Jack Welch, Sun Microsystems' Scott McNealy and Microsoft's Steve Ballmer are unapologetic about three things: one, providing everyone with resources and opportunity; two, clearly providing the best players with the greatest rewards; and three, insuring that chronic poor performers are shown the door.

Powell's concern about assessing and rewarding performance is such that he does not shirk from elevating it above any other consideration, even politically sensitive issues. For example, in a public forum within the State Department, an employee asked Powell point-blank about his commitment to diversity. Powell's response was equally point-blank:

> *I will be looking at promotion rates. I will be*
> *looking at what happens as you go up the*
> *cone, to make sure that there are no vestiges*
> *of institutional discrimination of any kind,*

and it's performance that counts. But I'm also
not going to blink if performance isn't there
but a claim is made because of diversity you
have to do this. Performance is going to
count. So we have to make the pool big
enough in the beginning so that performance
can count as you move up.

"LEADING ANGER" IS ESSENTIAL FOR SUCCESS

In the aftermath of the September 11 terrorist attacks in New York and Washington, President Bush and his cabinet—the nation's leaders—found themselves in an extremely difficult situation. No matter which course of action they chose, they were almost certain to anger an important constituency, either in this nation or abroad.

Good leaders in any enterprise know that this dilemma comes with the territory. Any significant leadership decision will get some people mad.

Further, the more stressful the conditions faced by the enterprise, the bolder the leadership decisions needed. The bolder the decision, the more it upsets the status quo. The more it upsets the status quo, the further likelihood that some (or many) people will be angry.

And yet, when the enterprise faces turbulent and stressful times, a nondecision from the leader might very well generate the most universal anger. (Can you imagine Americans' reactions if the Bush team would have been perceived as indecisive or waffling in the wake of September 11?) One can argue that the weakest leaders get everybody mad. If a leader doesn't provide the boldness and inspiration that capable employees (or citizens) yearn for, the resulting disappointment is enough to demoralize the entire enterprise—whether nation or corporation.

In the first days after the September 11 tragedy, Powell riled some people within the Bush administration by arguing for goal clarification, even at the expense of immediate action. What, exactly, are we trying to achieve? Once those goals are defined, what roles might diplomacy and military play in achieving them?

Then, even as he mounted an intensive diplomatic coalition-building effort, he was not afraid to rile potential allies either. Within 48 hours of the September 11 attack, Powell telephoned Pakistani leader General Pervez Musharraf and told him bluntly: "General, you have got to make a choice." Within the next 24 hours Powell had dispatched Deputy Secretary Richard Armitage to deliver a seven-point ultimatum to Musharraf demanding, among other things, that Pakistan close its border with Afghanistan, open its intelligence files to the U.S., and provide safe haven for American forces. Clearly, the Bush administration sweetened the deal with a quid pro quo of political and economic aid, but the point is that Powell was not hesitant to risk upsetting or offending a potentially critical ally.

The recent terrorist attacks have been interpreted—I think correctly—as an indicator of enormous *change*. It's too early to say exactly how that change will manifest itself in our professional and private lives, but it's safe to say that we will think about ourselves, and about our challenges and opportunities, very differently from here on out. The rules of engagement have changed in fundamental ways. It won't be "business as usual" anytime in the foreseeable future.

Many managers had reached similar conclusions about the business world well before the events of September 11. Across a wide spectrum of industries, they perceived a melting away of the status quo and a rewriting of the rules. They talked a great deal about change, which became by far the most popular theme of corporate pep rallies and management retreats in the 1990s.

Well, that was good as far as it went. But in all likelihood far too few managers *acted* on the perceived need for change. All too often, they fell back on what leadership researcher James O'Toole calls the "ideology of comfort and the tyranny of custom." Why? The answer, I believe, is simple: change doesn't happen because custom is powerful, comfort is comfortable, and managers are *afraid to piss people off* in their quest to change things for the better.

Too often, even in companies that are in dire straits, managers find it difficult to squarely confront (however constructively) employees, peers, or partners whose performance is subpar or is no longer appropriate for the times. Nor can they bear to rile them by challenging their ingrained power fiefdoms, by unabashedly lauding and promoting new people who hold contrarian ideas, or by following through on sweeping changes to tradition.

They should heed the example of Colin Powell. They should set a clear agenda, and act decisively if it's the right thing to do for the enterprise. They should continually clarify, exhort and push. They should confront employees, peers or partners whose performance is below par or no longer appropriate for a changed business context. They should reward differentially.

Those managers who fail to carry out these responsibilities are putting their organization in harm's way. In the hope of not getting people angry, they're not sufficiently raising the bar on performance, or sparking the changes, both in direction and in urgency, that are absolutely necessary for their organization's revitalization and success.

SUMMARY

On one level, the practical lesson for leaders is straightforward: Set a clear disruptive agenda, stick to it, invite everyone to participate, give them considerable opportunity to shape and develop it, provide people with tools and resources to succeed, be open and collaborative, hold people fully accountable for new results, and reward accordingly. That's what it means to be responsible, and "being responsible sometimes means pissing people off."

On another level, the lesson is deeper. Good leaders don't evade or cover up anger, they lead it. Powell will tell you that when leaders press for new directions, new behaviors, and new performance expectations, peoples' comfort zones will be invaded, and they'll get angry. *And that's precisely what's supposed to happen.*

Ultimately, a good leader knows that gaining respect is more important than being liked, and performance is more important than popularity. That being said, earning people's respect and insuring top performance is the surest way to earn loyalty and, yes, even affection. And when you're asking people to take risks for you—in the case of the military, to risk death for you—respect and performance are indispensable resources indeed.

POWELL PRINCIPLES

1. **Make performance and change top organizational priorities.** Elevating performance and challenging the status quo are two keys to success. Help others do the same. Provide people with the tools, technologies, and training to build their skill sets and enhance their level of personal responsibility. Help people jettison habits and mindsets

that don't work anymore. Encourage experimentation and innovative initiatives to replace "the old way." Encourage a culture of constant curiosity and innovation, in which sacred cows are pushed toward extinction.

2. **Define the new game, and expect everyone to play it.** Clearly articulate a broad agenda (priorities, goals, values), and provide everyone with the tools and training necessary to take powerful action. Insist that everyone take the responsibility for carving out the best ways to execute that agenda.

3. **Make sure that your best performers are more satisfied than your poor performers.** Reward those who demonstrate commitment to your new agenda. Remember that this is not a zero-sum game, and that there's plenty for everyone, as long as performance counts. But don't take the easy, "across-the-board" way out.

4. **Get rid of nonperformers.** Powell, like other effective leaders, confronts people who can't or won't perform. Tightly run organizations can't afford foot-draggers, who not only consume resources, but get in the way of (or, worse, demoralize) the high achievers around them.

5. **Consider the possibility that if nobody's pissed off, you may not be pushing hard enough.** I think this is the implicit lesson behind the lesson of this chapter. No, random hostilities are not what the organization needs. But Powell's example suggests that a commitment to creative disruption ought to be at the heart of your leadership style.

CHAPTER 2

PROMOTE A CLASH OF IDEAS

*"The day soldiers stop bringing
you their problems is the day
you have stopped leading them."*

TO INTRODUCE THIS CHAPTER, I want to tell a story that grows out of a one-on-one session I had with Colin Powell. The meeting took place in the spring of 2000, about a year before he took over as secretary of state. I arrived at the designated building in Alexandria, Virginia, and made my way through the sequence of obligatory checkpoints. Finally, I was ushered in to meet the nation's former number-one soldier, then in the seventh year of what he euphemistically referred to as his "retirement." In fact, he was anything but retired. At that time, he was actively involved in his America's Promise foundation, was serving on several high-profile corporate and institutional boards, and was one of the most sought-after public speakers in the world. He was, by almost any conceivable measure, a larger-than-life figure.

So I wasn't particularly surprised to see that his office was quite spacious, and that his desk was nothing short of vast. What *did* surprise me, though, was the speed with which Powell abandoned the monumental piece of furniture. He bounded up, moved quickly around the desk, shook my hand warmly, and ushered me into a smallish alcove adjoining his office. The alcove contained only a small round table and a few chairs. As we seated ourselves, I guessed that any meeting with Powell in this little corner of his office was likely to be an intimate one. There wasn't *room* for any other kind of meeting.

My guess soon proved correct. We sat in that small alcove, with our feet and knees nearly bumping, and had a far-ranging discussion of history, books, travel, money, family—and, of course, leadership. From the start, I felt entirely at home. That was partly because he was a welcoming host, but it was also because of the impact of that odd table, stuck in that intimate little corner. In part because of the physical surroundings, I felt that I was getting to know him, and that I was free to speak my mind honestly.

Some of what Powell said at that session confirmed my reading of the situation. He explained to me that he thrives on—in fact, *depends* upon—honest dialogue. When he was a military leader, he wanted soldiers of any rank to understand that when they met with him, he genuinely wanted to hear what was on their mind. It was a habit that he carried forward into private life, he said, and I'm sure it's a habit he later took with him to the State Department.

Parking yourself behind a massive desk, Powell told me, is a very effective barrier to candid communication. (In his long career, he had encountered lots of little people hiding behind big desks.) Holding a meeting at a small, round table, by contrast, sends a very different message. It suggests accessibility, egalitarianism, and safety, and it fosters a sense of trust.

Lest the reader conclude that I'm deeply interested in office furniture, let me emphasize that to me, a table is little more than an assembly of wood and nails. It's the philosophy behind the table that interests me. The table in Powell's office had a particular impact because it embodied a principle that is central to his entire management philosophy: *accessibility*. Simply put, the leader has a responsibility to be available to his troops. He or she has to give them an easy opportunity to speak their piece, without fear of bureaucratic or personal retribution.

And good things follow from that availability. In his autobiography, Powell tells a story about how he took pains to be accessible to the troops during his Army command. Every afternoon, he walked the same route at the same time, deliberately setting himself up to be "ambushed" (his word). It wasn't long before people with problems realized that this was a golden opportunity to get the boss's ear—and they took full advantage of that opportunity.

At the same time, Powell adds, he made it clear to his immediate subordinates that he had no intention of using his little strolls to undermine the chain of command. (As he well knew, in the military, respect for the chain of command can mean the difference between life and death.) This was, he emphasized, simply a good way for people to blow off steam, and perhaps even convey a great idea in an unfiltered form. The noncommissioned and junior officers got the point and stopped worrying about open lines from the bottom of the pyramid to the top. "If anything," Powell recalls, "my outdoor office hours gave them a chance to blow off steam, too."

But the daily stroll served as more than just a relief valve. It also served as a kind of mirror that each day was being held up to the management of the organization. As Powell puts it:

> *The day soldiers stop bringing you their problems is the day you have stopped leading them. They have either lost confidence that you can help them or concluded that you do not care. Either case is a failure of leadership.*

As I suggested in Chapter 1, the author of these blunt and challenging words is not doing his daily rounds in an effort to be a nice guy. Nor is he making any commitment to act on anything he might happen to hear. (No organization can act on every good idea that comes its way, and an organization certainly shouldn't rush to pursue the *bad* ideas.) Nor, as I see it, is he limiting himself to simply addressing soldiers' immediate dissatisfactions. His point is much deeper: namely, that we are in a global knowledge economy, and that to succeed in that economy, a leader must blow the communications lid off the place. He or she must encourage an *active, continuing* communication of concerns, observations, data, insights, and suggestions from and among employees.

What's needed, in other words, is a purposeful clash of ideas.

ENCOURAGE A "NOISY SYSTEM"

A few years ago, Powell made the following observation:

> *What will make things different in the 21st century is that the world is going through a transformation—a transformation that affects the industrial world as well as the political and economic world. . . . The world is being fundamentally reshaped by the information and technology revolution, which is supplanting the industrial revolution.*

In that kind of world, Powell argues, *ideas matter*. Ideas build up, or bring down, empires. Speaking in early 2001 to State Department personnel, for example, Powell explained the collapse of the Soviet empire in the following terms: "We beat them on the field of ideas; we contained them on the field of battle but we beat them on the field of ideas. . . . Even in places like Iraq and Iran and elsewhere, I believe these forces are irresistible."

So to be successful, leaders must consciously work to stay in touch with the best ideas of the people they lead. Hasn't the organization invested considerable resources in the recruitment and training of these good people? Well, then, the organization ought to get the benefit of that investment. Its leaders ought to be constantly on the lookout for great ideas. And at the risk of stating the obvious, this effort has to go far beyond the confines of the traditional suggestion box. The organization's leaders have to use their every capacity to reach out. Straight-ahead vision is good; so is peripheral vision. I once talked to a leader who felt that it was his job to "smell" what was going on in his organization.

Great leaders also use this process to help their people *articulate their issues*. I wasn't on those daily walks that Powell took through his brigades, but I have no doubt that he actively engaged with those people who ambushed him. I'm sure he responded substantively, and I'm sure they responded in kind. Through this kind of dialogue—and, obviously, through more formal processes of follow-up—an urge becomes an initiative, and an impulse turns into a "skunk works."

So it's not just a process of installing the relief valve mentioned previously, and it's not just a way to harvest ideas. It's also a process of involving people in and making them take responsibility for the shaping of their ideas. Yes, by opening

up the pipeline, the leader may well unleash a flood of interesting and provocative insights. But the ultimate goal is to
inspire people in the organization not just to *voice* problems,
but also to figure out ways to *solve* problems.

In days gone by, a country's size and location, combined
with its natural resources, largely determined its wealth and
power. Until fairly recently, the same could be said of a company—but no longer. Today, a company's physical or financial assets are far less important to its success than its idea
base. The key question is, how many fresh, innovative,
shared, implementable ideas are bubbling away in the corporate cauldron? And, just as important, how accessible are
those ideas? Can they float up to the top of the pot without
being scrubbed, sanitized, and spun?

This is what's on Powell's mind when he advocates for
what he calls "a noisy system," characterized by a clash of
ideas. Consider the following pronouncement, which was one
of the first that he made to his new staff at State:

> *You will find an open style, you will find me*
> *bouncing in, you will find me wanting to talk*
> *to desk officers. I want to hear the rough*
> *edges of all arguments. I don't want to*
> *concur things to death and coordinate things*
> *to death so I get a round pebble instead of a*
> *stone that has edges on it. I want to hear*
> *from you, I want to get all the great ideas*
> *that exist throughout the Department.*

Maybe this sounds like motherhood and apple pie. In all
too many companies, though, important decisions are still
made behind closed doors, with surprisingly limited input
from below. (And the information that *does* make its way up

the ladder often looks more like pebbles than like stones.) Vital information is still hoarded at specific levels in the management hierarchy, or within functional silos. An astonishingly large volume of information is unnecessarily—even stupidly—marked "top secret," "need-to-know basis," or "for your eyes only." In many cases, the organization is so walled up that the best people in Department A effectively have no idea of what their skilled counterparts in Department B are doing.

Small wonder, then, that so many organizations fail to adapt. Sure, the concept of clashing opinions implies controversy, aggravation, and maybe even some pain. But without clashing opinions, organizations stagnate. They atrophy from the extremities inward. (This is one reason why the people at the core are often the last to learn about a serious problem.) So the organization needs to use noisy systems and creative clashes to pump up its own pulse—and, of course, its leaders need to keep a finger squarely on that pulse.

POWELL'S THREE COMMUNICATION SECRETS

Let's look more closely at some of the specific things that Powell does to make sure that robust lines of communication—*candid* communication—are woven into the fabric of the enterprise.

- *Powell deliberately encourages and solicits communication between temporary equals in order to create a more open culture.*

Here is how he explained it in a recent interview:

> **When a captain came in to see me, I would tell the youngster to sit down. I'd say, Talk to me, son. What have you got? And then I'd let**

him argue with me. I would do everything
I could to let him think he was arguing
with an equal, because he knew more
about the subject than I did.

Again, this doesn't mean that Powell automatically agreed with the captain's premises or prescriptions. But putting rank to one side, he listened as hard as he could to an individual who was very likely to be in the know. He listened, and he frequently learned.

In the same spirit, in the late 1980s, he asked some of the privates under his command if they had any bright ideas about how the coalition that was then being assembled worldwide might improve its chances of winning the operation that became known as Desert Storm. Powell is like an expert fisherman who refuses to fish only where the tour guides point him. He is constantly trolling for fresh angles and unfiltered knowledge, preferably from sources that are closer to the trenches than he is.

Some readers might dismiss Powell's actions as irrelevant and "soft." Quite the contrary. Relevant information and employee commitment are keys to competitive success these days for any enterprise. Leaders who truly welcome a clash of ideas are hardly soft; they must be strong and sincere, especially when new ideas collide with their own. In today's State Department, John Bolton is the undersecretary of state for arms control and international security. His views are decidedly more hawkish than Powell's. Yet rather than marginalize him, Powell uses Bolton to challenge and refine his own thinking. For Powell, an open culture that encourages a healthy constructive clash of ideas is essential.

It is important to stress that all this is about *real* intelligence gathering, as opposed to manipulation or symbolism. Having said that, I'll add that Powell fully understands that the value of his actions extends far beyond his own conversations with captains and privates. Those conversations are a culture creator as well. "I also knew," Powell says of the hypothetical captain whom he encouraged to argue with him, "that when he got back to his office, he'd tell his friends that he had argued with the chairman of the Joint Chiefs of Staff....Word would spread. People would understand that when they came into my office, I really wanted to hear what they thought."

At the same time, those who were "boss watching" Powell would get a strong signal that behaving in this same way themselves might be a good idea—and this is one way in which culture begins to get built (or rebuilt). If the leader's example is clear enough and powerful enough, the organization gradually adopts that model. If the leader models straightforward communication, then the barriers that tend to inhibit communication start coming down. Listening, coaching, and supporting become the preferred leadership styles. Ideas in the organizational cauldron start bubbling upwards and sideways with greater speed and intensity, and cohesion and esprit de corps rise alongside them.

As chairman of the Joint Chiefs of Staff, Powell implemented other practices that were designed to enhance free and open communication. For example, he stopped putting out written agendas before meetings, in an effort to prevent well-meaning staffers from writing up position papers that their superiors would then recite at the table. And in a counterintuitive move, he closed the meetings of the Joint Chiefs of Staff to note takers, on the theory that his colleagues would speak more freely if their every word were not being recorded for posterity.

Even more dramatic is what Powell did when he first took over as chairman of the Joint Chiefs. He inherited a structure called the Chairman's Staff Group, comprised of two- and

three-star generals from the individual services who essentially combined, filtered and homogenized the services' advice
and information flowing to the chairman. In his first day on
the job, Powell called the members of this "Staff Group" and
told them: "Here's the drill: You're out of it." From then on,
Powell communicated directly with the young officers
assigned to him by the services. This step not only boosted
accessibility, timeliness and accuracy of information flow—
but it also sent a signal through the ranks about the kind of
open culture that Powell wanted under his helm.

- *Powell is acutely aware of the power of symbols to promote (or
  obstruct) communication.*

I mentioned the little round table that set the tone for my
conversation with Powell. But there are dozens (or hundreds,
or thousands) of such symbols that are under the leader's
control. In Powell's words:

> **In the military, when you become a four-star
> general, people will do anything you even
> suggest you want. If you say a wall looks a
> little dirty, by sundown it's painted. You have
> to be very careful what you say. I had to work
> at breaking down that deference to hear from
> my people. All the tables in my office and
> conference rooms were round so that there
> was never a head. I would always try not to
> wear my full uniform. I would always have
> my jacket and blouse with all the fruit salad
> on it thrown in the corner.**

The higher up the hierarchy one goes, Powell stressed to
me, the harder one has to work to stay in touch with real peo-

ple and real data. (Someone once made the same point by observing that the queen of England must think that all the world smells of fresh paint.) That's why Powell works at symbolism: as a way of leveraging himself.

It's also why:

- *Powell openly sidesteps rank, hierarchy, and red tape in order to open up communication.*

As we've already seen, Powell is perfectly willing to eliminate layers of bureaucracy to boost accessibility. Barring that, he often simply ignores them.

"He jumps over layers of bureaucracy," one State Department official has said, "to deal with people directly." When he visits foreign outposts, for example, he is likely to astonish some country desk officer by dropping by unannounced to talk a little business. Often, during official tours, he will carve out a segment of his daily calendar for private conversations with front-line people.

On the eve of President Bush's first foreign trip, to Mexico, Powell made a move that within the then-prevailing State Department culture constituted a revolutionary departure. He requested that a group of desk officers in Mexico City—"the people who do all the work," as he described them—meet with the president to "have a conversation" about Mexico.

The desk officers were amazed, and initially skeptical. In the State Department hierarchy, desk officers seldom briefed anyone higher than a deputy assistant secretary. Once they realized that Powell's invitation was genuine, however, they excitedly prepared briefs on politics, economics, energy, migration, narcotics, and border issues. The meeting, which was facilitated by Powell, began with these unprecedented presentations, and was followed by informal question-and-answer dialogues among the desk officers, Powell, Bush, and senior national security and State Department officials. By all accounts, it was a highly productive—as well as startling— departure from standard operating procedures.

Powell wasn't aiming for feel-goods or warm-and-fuzzies. He wanted, and got, a higher-quality conversation than would otherwise have taken place. He also wanted to raise the bar, and kick up performance expectations, for *everyone* at State. I'm sure that once the Mexico story got out on the department's grapevine, State personnel all over the world got the idea, and *fast*. Or, more accurately, they got two ideas: (1) Important people cared what they thought, and (2) it would be an excellent time to organize one's best thinking.

Powell extends this philosophy to resources outside his organization as well. Some leaders choose to keep outsiders— especially outsiders with a reputation for adversarialism—at arm's length. Powell seems determined to bring them into the tent and get the benefit of whatever insight they may possess. For example, while preparing for his visit to Africa in the first week of June 2001, he made a point of soliciting input from the Constituency for Africa (CFA), a Washington-based advocacy group focused on African issues.

The CFA had been a vocal and effective critic of America's Africa policies, and didn't seem like a potential ally of the Bush administration. But Powell recognized that this group had significant experience, expertise, contacts, and credibility with Africa and its leaders. He wanted to *access* that unusual resource. So he simply ignored protocol and invited them into the tent.

Some members of the Washington press corps took note of Powell's unusual tactics. "Instead of trying to make an end run around CFA," wrote DeWayne Wickham of *USA Today*, "Powell...listened to their concerns. As a result, they're working with him, rather than beating up on him."

Is there a private-sector equivalent? I think so. In recent years, many savvy private-sector executives have rethought the way they handle "outsiders." They have stopped thinking of the other entities in their supply chains as vultures and sharks. They have discovered that bringing suppliers, key customers, strategic partners, and (for specific ventures) even competitors into selected activities of the business can pay significant dividends in terms of innovation, cost efficiency, and market development.

LEVERAGE TECHNOLOGY TO SPEED COMMUNICATION

- *Powell emphasizes technology as a key tool in building open communication.*

One of the key themes that recurs throughout this book is Powell's understanding of, and commitment to, the digital economy. The Web has permeated and changed almost every key function of business, from back-office and human resources issues to supply-chain and customer-relations management.

Powell couldn't be more clear on this issue:

> **With the end of the Cold War came the explosion of the information and technology revolution, where not only did you have this mosaic, this kaleidoscope, but you see it all being connected together through the power of the Internet, and fax machines, and satellite dishes, and cellular telephony, all allowing us to move information, knowledge, data, capital around the world at the speed of light.... I am**

absolutely persuaded of the transformational nature of this new technology and what it is going to do to the world.

Powell is not simply persuaded; he is captivated. "I *love* the Internet!" he often exclaims. And as we will see in other chapters in this book, he's determined to make the Internet a key resource for managing the Department of State.

So what does this have to do with candid communication and a clash of ideas? Everything. The power of the Internet lies in its capacity to obliterate barriers to the flow of knowledge. Nowadays, anyone armed with a laptop can access almost anyone and anything, almost anywhere—and this information comes in a raw, unfiltered, unedited, uncensored form, more or less in real time.

And of course, this is not just a solo activity. Today, networks of individuals and organizations equipped with fairly basic hardware and software can collaborate in ways that were simply unimaginable in the past. People can link up in new ways, and use those links to spur exceptional accomplishments.

So in the context of an open organization structure and an inclusive culture—in other words, in the kind of climate that Powell advocates and fosters—technology can be truly liberating. But all the technology in the world won't much help an organization that restricts people's capacity to gain access to, and contribute to, the flow of ideas. Investing huge sums in state-of-the-art technology will produce little or no return if the organization remains psychologically or hierarchically closed. If leaders remain aloof from their employees, if managers hoard information in order to enhance their authority, or if the rank and file don't feel free to voice their honest opinions, then technology won't unleash the value-adding ideas and exchange that leaders seek.

*I'm looking for leaders in the public
diplomacy and public affairs empire who are
very much in tune with this new way of
communicating with people, who understand
how to take messages out in the
21st century ... because I believe it is
essential for us to spread freedom, to be
able to communicate it properly.*

Imagine an organization within which any employee can instantly access any colleague at any corporate outpost and receive immediate (or near-immediate) online input and consultation. Imagine an organization in which, with a few clicks of a mouse, an employee seeking a better sense of a competitive context can call up relevant information from data banks all across the organization. Well, these organizations exist today. And where they do, they are more a function of *culture* and *structure* than a function of the MIS budget or a particularly robust data pipeline. More than anything else, they are made possible by an open leadership style.

MAINTAIN ONE PURE, UNFILTERED LINE OF COMMUNICATION

It's time to tell one of my favorite Powell stories. The story involves one of his personal leadership tools, which I'll refer to as "The Phone." But first, a little background.

Being the chairman of the Joint Chiefs of Staff, Powell told me, is a strange experience. It is both liberating and inhibiting. Yes, the chairman has a personal staff of more than ninety people, including bodyguards, pilots, aides, office clerks, and housekeepers. As a result, there's not a lot that one has to do for oneself, in terms of the daily habits of living. And then, of course, there are the other 1,500 or so people who work on the Joint Chiefs' payroll. Every last one of them, said Powell, is devoted to making his or her superiors' lives easier.

And, Powell told me with a wry smile, every last one of these people was also dedicated to shielding him from information. Their impulse was understandable, even admirable: They wanted to spare their bosses the onerous task of shoveling through mountains of data, much of which was irrelevant to the tasks at hand. They condensed, filtered, and edited. And, as Powell came to see it, they wove a tight cocoon around their unsuspecting superiors.

So Powell invented The Phone. This was a private line that he had brought into his office. Only a few trusted friends and advisors—Powell's inner circle—knew the number. Everyone in this stable of intimates had his or her own reliable network across the vast establishment of the U.S. military—and, of course, in Washington. When these people had something interesting to say, they called him up. As Powell explained it:

> *They would tell me when I did something that made sense, when I screwed up, how people inside and outside the organization were reacting, what they were planning on doing about it, when I was going to get good news, and when I was in deep trouble.*

Nobody except Powell—not an aide, not his secretary— was allowed to answer The Phone. If it rang three times and nobody answered, the caller hung up and tried again later. Sometimes, when he was feeling the need for a little unvarnished truth telling, Powell would get on The Phone himself and start dialing members of his cadre.

It is noteworthy that no one else was permitted to answer The Phone. By inventing and enforcing that rule, Powell was making absolutely sure that his eyes and ears out there in the world wouldn't get "managed" by some well-meaning staffer. He was protecting the quality of the information flow—and, incidentally, making an important point to his office staff: *Good information is invaluable. If my actions or inactions are causing problems, I'm going to hear about them without the sugar coating.*

One really has to appreciate Powell's commitment to open cultures, unvarnished truth, and clash of ideas in order to understand that The Phone was not used in a malevolent Big Brother way, but as a means to keep him accurately apprised of the Good, Bad, and Ugly that he himself caused as captain of the ship.

LISTENING BEGETS LISTENING

In a conversation with Powell, you are likely to be struck by how intently he listens. In fact, he seems more inclined to listen than to be listened to.

Again, this reflects Powell's determination to learn whatever he can, wherever he can. But it is also another example of his modeling the behavior that he believes will foster better communication. Good listening begets good listening. Ideas get exchanged faster and more reliably.

Good listening also makes it far easier to deliver bad news. When Powell visited Africa for the first time in June 2001, he impressed African leaders with his obvious determination to hear and understand what they were saying. (Evidently, not all previous American visitors had listened this carefully.) His responses to their concerns, especially regarding the devastation that the AIDS virus was causing on their continent, were seen as clear evidence that they had been heard and understood.

In turn, the African leaders listened to some blunt talk from him. They wanted American investment dollars? Well, then, they had to change their ways. "Money is a coward," he told them. "Money does not go where it will not be safe, where it will not draw a return, and where people are ripping it off." It was the responsibility of leaders like themselves, he said, to create a stable investment climate in their home countries.

The American press corps expressed surprise at Powell's remarkable display of candor. The African leaders, for their part, indicated that they would take the American's tough words to heart. Clearly, they heard Powell's message because it was part of a dialogue—an exchange of ideas. If he had simply attempted to *lecture* them, he (and his ideas) would have gotten nowhere.

When managers ascend the corporate hierarchy, they sometimes become afflicted with a curious problem: Their ears get smaller, and their mouths get bigger. Perversely, the more they say without hearing, they less likely they are to be heard. Leaders who *shut up and listen* not only learn a lot, but often create an environment in which others are willing to listen to them.

SUMMARY

Open doors, an unfettered clash of ideas, an unfiltered dialogue, all aimed at solving problems in extraordinary ways and inspiring quantum improvements in performance— sounds great, right? Sounds like the target that all organizations ought to be shooting at?

The answer is obviously yes. But if we held senior managers up to this standard, many would fail. Many tolerate the barriers to communication that they inherited from their predecessors because they don't want to go against the grain of the status quo. Others erect new barriers, either wittingly or unwittingly. The result is a gradual erosion of organizational capabilities. The company stops innovating and stagnates, and no one can quite figure out why.

Great leaders are mold smashers. But they know that molds get smashed when innovation flourishes. That's why they continuously root out the barriers to communication and information flow and then demolish them. They set up new systems to short-circuit overly complicated organizational wiring. They demand candor. They create cultures in which exciting ideas bubble up freely.

They find ways to "smell" what's going on in their organizations. They keep their doors open. They stay in touch with people up and down the line. They help people understand their own ideas better, and they ensure that the organization can harvest the very best ideas that are out there, in every corner of the enterprise.

POWELL PRINCIPLES

1. **Maintain a real, no b.s. open-door policy.** The leader must encourage communication from every quarter. Remember Powell's warning: When people stop coming to you with their problems, this indicates a failure in leadership.

2. **Foster a "noisy system."** Get everyone to participate in the information flow. Encourage a diversity of opinion and what Powell calls a clash of ideas. In this age of uncertainty, leaders need to involve and engage every mind in the organization.

3. **Use every means to encourage communication, and never let rank or hierarchy get in the way.** Smoke out the opinions of those closest to the front lines. Invite outsiders

into the discussion. Don't be afraid to share information with the right constituencies.

4. **Use technology to improve communication.** Harness the power of new technologies in order to ensure that everyone is included. Invest the necessary resources—and, more important, create the psychological climate in which information flowing freely over networks is seen as a resource rather than a threat.

5. **Treat turf wars as the enemy of communication.** Knock down barriers. Reward those who follow suit. Punish those who try to put the barriers back up again. Beat this drum incessantly: *We're always better off being open and candid with each other.*

CHAPTER 3

THE
EGO TRAP

*"Never let your ego
get so close to your position
that when your position goes,
your ego goes with it."*

ONE OF THE PIVOTAL MOMENTS in Colin Powell's career was prompted by none other than Mikhail Gorbachev, the Soviet leader who, more than anyone else, was responsible for the dismantling of the U.S.S.R. In the spring of 1988, National Security Advisor Powell and Secretary of State George Shultz flew to Moscow to prepare for President Reagan's visit to the Soviet Union. During their first meeting, Premier Gorbachev looked across the table at Powell and, through his translator, delivered an unequivocal message: *General, I'm ending the Cold War, and you're going to have to find yourself a new enemy.*

In his years as a public speaker, Powell often built this story into his speeches. I once heard him confess to a corporate audience—with a good dose of self-effacing humor—that this was unwelcome news from the Soviet premier. The first words that came into his mind, he told his audience, were, "But I don't want to find a new enemy!" Why? It's simple: He'd invested twenty-eight years in this particular enemy. It was painful, Powell said, to realize that "everything I had worked against no longer mattered." The prospect of finding a new cause—of starting all over again—was daunting.

But as Gorbachev moved ahead with his purposeful unraveling of the Soviet empire, Powell acknowledged that he had no choice: He had to give up his tried-and-true adversary. Even harder, he had to protect his own sense of self-worth, purpose, and mission. Just because his enemy was disappearing, it didn't mean that *he* was disappearing.

The lesson he ultimately took away from this episode, he told his audience a decade later, was, *Never let your ego get so close to your position that when your position goes, your ego goes with it.* The lesson was crystallized, Powell went on to say, when he overheard a conversation between two lawyers in the Department of Energy. One had just lost an important case and was thoroughly dispirited. "Hey," said the other. "You lost the case, but you didn't lose *you.*"

As managers, so much of *who we are* is wrapped up in *what we do.* We carefully create the status quo, and then we become prisoners of it. Our self-esteem, our career histories, our enterprise infrastructures, our technologies, our cultures and traditions, our skill sets, our views of competitors, customers, and partners—all of these combine to make us who we are, at least in the workplace. And this is perfectly understandable. After all, humans are creatures of habit. Habits help us set limits on choice making. Habits make us predictable to our colleagues, and therefore easier to work with. Habits serve us well.

The problem arises, as Powell discovered in his conversation with Gorbachev, when our habits focus us primarily on the past. It's gratifying (and again human) to want to dwell on the marketplace of yesterday, where we fought good battles and enjoyed great victories. It's tempting to see the marketplace of today (and tomorrow) as being very much like the marketplace of the past.

Unfortunately, it can't be, and it won't be. Effective leaders, therefore, look beyond yesterday—and beyond today. They don't cling to familiar territory. They don't let their egos distort the organizational agenda. They look for a Gorbachev to tell them that their worldview is outdated. They ferret out clues to what tomorrow may look like. They use this information to set a new course, and to help others adjust their circumstances—both the individual and the corporate status quo—to reflect *tomorrow's* conditions.

CHANGE BEFORE YOU ARE FORCED TO CHANGE

Of course, Gorbachev didn't provide the only clue that the old world order (in which Powell had invested those twenty-eight years) was fading away. By the late 1980s, Powell was seeing many signs that truly massive changes were underway. Not only did the "evil empire" collapse, but the Warsaw Pact imploded, the Berlin Wall fell, and the ideologies of Marxism and Leninism sank into disrepute. Literally billions of people around the world embraced democracy and market economies for the first time.

What did all this change mean for the U.S. military, of which Powell became the senior military leader in 1989? The answer was not immediately obvious. Some people argued that the military should continue doing what it had been doing for decades. After all (this argument went), Russia and several of the other successor states to the Soviet Union were still nuclear powers. They were still autocratic and deeply suspicious regimes (as they had been for decades, or even centuries). The best strategy, these people argued, was to stay the course and upgrade what had been done in the past with improvements in quality, cost-efficiencies, and the like.

Powell listened hard to these arguments. He also listened hard to people on the other side of the debate, who said that the world had changed fundamentally, and that the U.S. military had to catch up with, and get ahead of, those enormous changes. When he became chairman of the Joint Chiefs of Staff, he made it clear that he agreed with the reformers, and that simply "staying the course," even with "continuous improvement" goals would be a prescription for irrelevance. Yes, he reasoned, the world was still a very dangerous place, and the United States still had multiple global responsibilities, some of which would need the force of military power to fulfill. So, clearly, there was an important place for the military. But, just as clearly, the military needed a new mission.

> *In the military, to put it in corporate terms,*
> *[the end of the Cold War meant that] our*
> *product line was now out of date.... I had to*
> *restructure in a way so that ... the new,*
> *smaller force, with a new mission, had the*
> *same quality and efficiency as the larger force*
> *and the same morale. And we did that.*

In late 1989, Powell, as chairman of the Joint Chiefs, wrote the following:

> *I saw it as my main mission to move the*
> *armed forces onto a new course, one parallel-*
> *ing what was happening in the world today,*
> *not one chained to the previous forty years.*

The vision that Powell and his colleagues inherited back in the late 1980s was of a Free World standing up to an Evil Empire. It was a monolithic, reductionist worldview: Everything that happened anywhere in the world could be traced back to, and explained by, the uncomplex ideologies of the Cold War. Most military planning keyed off of this monolithic vision. If we could just figure out the Soviets' next strategic move and block that move, the military analysts reasoned, our security would be assured. The next war, it was assumed, would look very much like the last war.

For example, as Powell recounts in his autobiography, the Cold War mission of the Navy included protecting the North Atlantic sea-lanes so that U.S. forces could get to Europe quickly and engage Warsaw Pact forces on the ground. This was a lesson that had been learned in World War II—fully fifty years earlier—and that no one had ever *unlearned*.

When we assumed the chairmanship in 1989, Powell was convinced that it was time to unlearn some lessons. Working with like-minded colleagues—but also giving his critics plenty of air time—Powell began shaping a vision that revolved around a leaner, nimbler, more mobile, technologically "smarter" military that could anticipate and put out fires from multiple sources around the world. He assumed that some of these fires would be small scale, and that they would involve new strategies and new kinds of weapons.

In the wake of the September 2001 terrorist attacks on New York and Washington, one could make the case that Powell and his colleagues underestimated the nature and scope of a transformation that was already under way. One could argue that they should have pushed harder and gone farther. But hindsight is proverbially 20/20. Powell deserves credit for both foresight and courage, in choosing more than a decade ago to deliver a message that few in the military wanted to hear. The move was courageous in part because few felt a sense of urgency. We had *won*, right? Why change the strategy that won the Cold War?

As Americans have now learned so painfully, the so-called first war of the twenty-first century is being fought under entirely new rules of engagement. The enemy is not a nation, or an organization, or an individual. The enemy is borderless, shrouded in secrecy, and "virtual." The goals, and even the mindset, of the enemy's foot soldiers are unfathomable to many Westerners. Most often, the combatants will fight not in the daylight, but in the shadows.

And although Powell no longer has responsibility for military planning, he still has strong opinions on the subject of national security in changing circumstances. He argues today that the United States needs a new multidimensional mix of military and nonmilitary initiatives. This, in turn, requires us to involve ourselves in new kinds of missions, organizations, allies, weapons, technologies, intelligence gathering, law enforcement, and diplomacy.

That sounds almost self-evident, does it not? But consider an article that appeared in the *Wall Street Journal* on September 19, 2001, just a week after the World Trade Center and Pentagon disasters. Even though the U.S. armed forces will be receiving up to an additional $17 billion, reported the *Journal*, "it's not clear whether the new money will go toward truly changing the way the Pentagon does business—or instead, pay for the same kinds of high-priced tanks, planes, and ships that the military brass, the defense industry, and Congress have championed in the past. While the Pentagon has indicated its intention to engineer a major shift over the long term, it already faces pressure from defenders of the status quo."

So let's recapitulate. Even after Powell's initiatives of the late 1980s and early 1990s, and even after a decade's worth of accumulating evidence that the military needed to change, and even after the horrific punctuation on September 11, 2001, there is *still* a chance that the additional $17 billion that was shaken loose by that tragedy will wind up supporting the military's traditional ways of doing business!

In the private sector, companies often turn a blind eye toward a changing environment. They circle the wagons to protect existing products, processes, sunk costs, and habits. Why? Because the status quo is enormously powerful. People invest in the status quo, both personally and professionally. They build up their current enemies, and then they become dependent on those enemies. The health of their egos becomes linked, in a perverse way, with the health of their enemies.

In such circumstances, expert and energetic leadership is needed. Great leaders in business continually press for new positions. They do so not just in times of crisis, when it's relatively easy (and often too late) to get most people to check their egos at the door, but also when things seem to be motoring along just fine—and, yes, even if the financials look good. They find ways to share their own sense of urgency.

In the following Powell quote, try replacing the word *Russia* with a noun from almost any competitive business sector. For example, take out *Russia* and insert *the mainframe*, or *the eight-track player*, or *the carburetor*, or *protectionism*, or, simply, *your currently accepted business model*. Powell's strong statement assumes new urgency:

> **First, you need to understand that Russia
> is not coming back. But you can't have a
> vacuum of mission. That leads to anxiety and
> dread. Dig deep and rip out that old mission
> and fill it immediately with a new mission**

and then start training for it.
You cannot tolerate a vacuum!

CHECK YOUR EGO

Good leaders have healthy egos—sometimes even *way* healthy egos. And that's more or less a necessity: Leaders have to possess a strong sense of self, and a strong *pride* of self, to do what they do. "When I get up in the morning," a CEO once said to me, "I feel a responsibility for 55,000 families." That takes nerve, self-assurance, and a steady hand. And, of course, the CEO almost never acts alone. A strong ego is also needed to mobilize teams in support of exceptional goals. So ego is a good and necessary asset in a leader.

The learning point, made earlier in the Powell-Gorbachev story, is that *leaders can't wed their egos to the status quo, because the status quo inevitably changes.* Great leaders take a deep breath, then walk right up to change and shake its hand. They check their egos and try on a new self-image. And when it comes to the people around them, they use the power of their egos to inspire and instigate change, rather than to resist it.

I believe that leaders nowadays ought to embrace Powell's lesson on ego with a real sense of urgency. Waves of social and economic change—big waves, powerful waves—are already crashing on the beach and splashing over the seawall. Managers who cling to their established positions and standard operating procedures will place their enterprises in jeopardy.

We will need to work together well because
we have a great challenge before us. But it is
not a challenge of survival anymore; it is a
challenge of leadership. For it is not a dark

*and dangerous ideological foe we confront as
we did for all those years, but now it is the
overwhelming power of millions of people
who have tasted freedom. It is our own
incredible success, the success of the values
that we hold dear, that has given us the
challenges that we now face.*

REINVENT YOUR JOB BEFORE IT'S TOO LATE

When managers lock their egos into a fixed position—by which I mean both job and mindset—they not only jeopardize their enterprises, but also jeopardize their own careers. The simple fact is that no matter who we are, *our jobs are becoming obsolete.* The skill sets and habits that we call upon to do our work are a little less valuable every day.

So unless we're ready to withdraw from the field and retire, we have to seize the initiative. Believe me: Whoever you are and whatever you do, someone out there is gunning for you (or at least for the resources that you control). We therefore have to continually reinvent our jobs, and make obsolete some or all of our accustomed activities, before someone else does. And if we are leaders of organizations, we have to create a climate in which we value people according to their ability to learn new skills and grab new responsibilities, thereby perpetually reinventing their jobs.

*This world is changing so much. And I have
got to make sure that the State Department is
on top of it, and I have got to make sure I am
pedaling as fast as the corporate world is
pedaling, the non-profit world is pedaling,
the advocacy world is pedaling.*

In such a climate, the most important question in performance evaluations is no longer, "How well have you performed your job since the last time we met?" Instead, it's, "How much have you *changed* your job?" What exciting new initiatives have you launched? What new projects have you started? How many cross-disciplinary action teams have you been invited to join? What innovative steps have you taken to boost efficiency, customer service, quality, or sales? What new skills and competencies have you learned, and how have you applied them to improving things around here? Which of last year's job responsibilities have you delegated, outsourced, automated, or eliminated, and what new responsibilities have you snared?

When leaders ask questions like that, they help to ensure that people's egos aren't entangled with their current titles or job descriptions. And people who can *answer* those kinds of questions assure themselves of growth, development, and authority within their organizations.

SUMMARY

Powell warns against getting stuck in one's position. Specifically, his advice is: Be flexible, be willing to change your opinions in light of new facts, and don't get hung up on any particular course of action if it's not essential to your mission. On top of that, be willing to question and change your mission when new "enemies" arise.

One level down, I think, Powell is arguing that one's ego can be either an asset or a liability on the path to success. Leaders help avoid stagnation—in their people and in their enterprises—by helping people optimally apply their egos to change, both in the marketplace and within the organization.

Leaders understand that "checked egos" make certain kinds of communications easier, and can make the group collectively far more productive. While working in the Reagan administration, for example, Powell got to know Ken Duberstein, the White House chief of staff. According to Powell, Duberstein had a gift for getting the members of the White House staff (some of whom were no doubt blessed with healthy egos) to get beyond their own passions and agendas and work together. The resulting work environment was highly collegial, productive, and fun.

When Powell wrote about not getting stuck in one's position in his memoirs, his advice to the reader was: Be willing to change your opinions in light of new facts, and don't get hung up on any particular course of action if it's not essential to your mission. Good advice, to be sure.

But as is the case with every chapter in this book, Powell's advice has rich multiple layers. I believe that the real power of managing egos is twofold. First, to help people avoid stagnation and paralysis in themselves and their enterprises. Second, to help people creatively apply their "egos" in new directions in order to capitalize on the constant changes in the external marketplace and the internal organization. So whether it's charting a course of action for one's enterprise, or charting a course of action for one's career, Powell's advice is useful indeed.

To conclude, I might add that Powell walks the talk on his advice to the "nth degree": A May 21, 2001 *U.S. News & World Report* blurb says that "It's the little things that have State Department workers cooing over their boss, Colin Powell. Their latest brag: Powell does his own photocopying and gets on his hands and knees to fix the machine when it jams."

Now there's someone who *literally* doesn't let his ego get too close to his position!

POWELL PRINCIPLES

1. **Look past today, and monitor the environment for tomorrow**. Don't get stuck in the past. Even in the best of weather, look for competitive clues on the horizon. Adapt to new situations, and, after embracing change, respond to it with innovative action.

2. **Challenge the prevailing wisdom.** What are the data telling you? Is it the same thing that your gut is telling you? If not, why not? What are those sea-lanes really going to look like in the war we're most likely to fight?

3. **Guard against competitive myopia.** Change your model before someone else changes it for you. The corporate graveyard is full of organizations that failed to take pre-emptive action.

4. *Make* **change** *mean* **growth.** Humans resist change. Change precipitates growth. Therefore, humans resist growth—even though it's growth that will keep them happily and gainfully employed. So leaders need to connect these dots in more constructive ways. Make *change* equivalent to *growth*, and make *growth* equivalent to *satisfaction*. Apply this lesson to your own career and personal development—regularly.

CHAPTER 4

DON'T GO
LOOKING FOR "NO"

*"You don't know what
you can get away with
until you try."*

COLIN POWELL is a methodical person. He analyzes his circumstances, and he understands the rules of the game that he's playing. At the same time, however, he doesn't hesitate to push things to the limit when the situation warrants it. He doesn't hesitate to work *around* the rules of the game creatively, without exactly breaking them. This is an important lesson—particularly in large organizations, where bureaucracies all too often rule the day.

There are numerous examples from Powell's career that make the point. While he was in a degree program at the National War College, Powell learned that he was to be assigned to the command of the 101st Airborne Unit, based at Fort Campbell, Kentucky, after graduating. Heading up the elite 101st Airborne was a plum assignment, and he was happy to get it. The plan hit a snag, however, when the then-commander of the 101st Airborne was promoted to brigadier general two months ahead of schedule, so that the unit was in need of a new commander immediately. The War College, however, had a policy of not allowing students to leave early. Powell was told that he would have to either turn down the assignment or give up his degree.

Neither option suited him. So he developed a solution that could satisfy each bureaucracy by bending the rules of both. Instead of taking the international field trip that traditionally occurred toward the end of one's stint at the War College, Powell arranged to visit a less exotic destination: Fort Campbell, Kentucky. This got him in the neighborhood of his hoped-for command, but the Infantry Branch announced that it would not let Powell assume command on *temporary* duty while he was still on *permanent* duty with the War College. Undaunted, Powell told them to put him on *permanent* command duty and on *temporary* duty with the War College. The strategy was highly unusual, but it worked. Powell assumed command of the 101st Airborne, and graduated from the War College six weeks later.

Powell also resorted to unorthodox methods during his White House Fellowship days. He was then serving as assistant to Fred Malek, the deputy director of the Office of Management and Budget. Malek asked Powell to figure out a way to reduce the number of career bureaucrats on the OMB staff in order to make room for new recruits. The problem was that these individuals couldn't be fired. Powell, stepping around a few rules and procedures, called a number of other agency officials in the White House and congratulated them on Malek's decision to transfer certain individuals to their agencies. Only after those officials were on board did Powell let slip that unfortunately, neither their positions nor their funding would be accompanying them. Mission accomplished—although again, in a way that sidestepped almost all bureaucratic protocols.

Note that in both cases Powell was not operating as a four-star general or CEO but rather a middle-level manager. He succeeded because he didn't look for a "no," and he didn't ask for a "yes."

In most organizations above a certain level of complexity, if you ask for permission to do something new and interesting (or even to do something conventional in an unconventional way), you're very likely to wind up banging your head against a wall. You're almost certain to run into someone who will attempt to dilute, postpone, or deep-six your initiative. We've talked about the (negative) power of the status quo. When people gain a sinecure in what appears to be a safe and stable organization, they often feel that it's their job to *keep things exactly as they are*. They decide that it's part of their job description to say no to anything innovative. This helps to explain why organizational inertia is such a chronic problem and so widespread in bureaucracies large and small.

To be sure, many organizations today are preaching the gospel of "empowerment" and "pushing authority down the hierarchy or chain of command." But if you look behind the words, these supposedly aired-out hierarchies are seldom much more empowering than your average bureaucracy. Yes, there may be a bit more freedom here and there, but this only underscores how much farther these organizations have to go before they are *truly* loosened up—before people will take even modest risks for the benefit of the enterprise.

So what's a motivated manager to do when he or she is stuck in such a situation? I suggest that managers consider a pithy observation by Colin Powell:

> *You don't know what you can*
> *get away with until you try.*

In other words, push things to the limit. Stretch the envelope. Don't ask for permission. Do what needs to be done. Do *something*.

PUSHING THE ENVELOPE SEPARATES THE GOOD FROM THE BAD

Maybe that advice will strike some readers as naïve or idealistic. If so, it's worth considering some empirical research that my colleague Linda Mukai and I conducted about a decade ago. We asked senior managers at five major corporations to identify two groups: their best middle managers, and their run-of-the-mill middle managers. Then Linda and I conducted interviews to determine what separated one group from the other.

We quickly learned that factors such as education, tenure, age, and sex were not key determinants. What *really* separated the two groups, it turned out, was *how likely a manager was to push things to the limit*. The mediocre managers basically carried out standing orders and passively waited for new orders to come down the pipe. Sometimes they complained about the unfairness, irrelevance, or vagueness of a given directive—but even against their better judgment, they still implemented it. Either way, they were mainly passive. They rarely initiated unorthodox actions on their own.

In contrast, the best managers were constantly skirting the edge, or leaning out beyond the edge, of their job descriptions and official responsibilities. They stretched the envelope, quite often without asking anybody's permission. They experimented, regularly trying out new things with their teams. They tinkered and explored, always with an eye toward improving something or toward moving the team closer to achieving an objective. Without being irresponsible or openly insubordinate, they bypassed procedures and the chain of command to get the job done.

In other words, the less effective middle managers were inclined to say, "If I haven't explicitly been told yes, I can't do it." The best ones were inclined to say, "If I haven't explicitly been told no, I *can* do it." There's a world of difference between these two worldviews.

This research was conducted way back in the late 1980s. Although I haven't revisited this particular topic since that time, I'm sure that things would shake out in much the same way today—and probably more so. To the extent that business has accelerated and competition has intensified in the intervening decade, people who don't elicit no's have only become more valuable.

So far, I've focused on the up-the-ladder implications of avoiding no's. It's also worth mentioning the down-the-ladder implications. If you simply conduct yourself as an obedient soldier, you'll eventually lose credibility with your team. If a leader's constant refrain is, "Sorry, great idea, but we can't try it because I haven't been given the go-ahead," his or her own credibility and authority suffer. Conversely, if a leader is willing to take calculated risks that will (1) help the larger organization and (2) let his or her own troops shine, that leader is likely to gain extraordinary performance and loyalty from those people.

STRETCHING: NOT JUST FOR CEOS

According to Powell, effective leaders create an environment in which people feel that they themselves have both the authority and the *obligation* to push the envelope:

*Generate the interest of 'the led,' so that they
contribute to the work of the organization
and want to be part of what's going on.*

Powell accomplishes this by surrounding himself with
good people, delegating extensively, and making it clear that
he expects people to find their own running room. For example, in the wake of the bombings of the U.S. embassies in
Kenya and Tanzania in 1998, Congress allocated more than
$1 billion for major security improvements to U.S. embassy
buildings around the world. The Foreign Buildings
Operations (FBO) office, the embassies' federal "landlord,"
was expected to take the lead in effecting these improvements. But the track record of FBO (then part of the Bureau
of Administration, which was in turn part of the State
Department) did not inspire a lot of confidence. Its projects
tended to be poorly planned, exceeded their budgets, and
often fell behind schedule.

When Powell took over at State, he was understandably
concerned that the FBO would not spend the congressional
appropriation wisely. Accordingly, he spun Foreign Buildings
off as an independent unit and turned over the reins to retired
Army Corps of Engineers Major General Charles Williams.
Williams's charge from Powell: *Do whatever is needed to over-
haul the capital planning procedures and operations of your
office.*

It was a clear and compelling mandate: As long as you stay
within your allocated budget and follow the broad guidelines
that you and I have agreed upon, Powell told Williams, you
are free to attack the problem in ways you deem appropriate.
Go ahead and push the envelope, bypass entrenched processes and habits, ignore traditions that don't work any more—
and whatever you do, *don't bother asking for permission.*

This requires the striking of a somewhat delicate balance. Powell wants to give people the space to try things without asking his permission, but at the same time, he doesn't want to discourage people from having a dialogue with him. So on the one hand, he takes care to tell his people that "sharing a problem [won't] be seen as weakness or failure, but as a sign of mutual confidence." But in almost the same breath, he stresses that people do not have to "buck every decision up to me."

The military was an interesting setting for this management style. The military *defines* the command-and-control hierarchical approach that permeated American companies for most of the twentieth century (and that still holds great sway today). So when Powell asserted that not every decision had to be bucked up to him—a giant step in the habits of some—he had to lay out some baby steps that illustrated what he was talking about. He took people down the path of autonomy little by little, first by saying things like, "I personally don't care if you hold reveille at 5:30 or 5:45 a.m.—and by the way, I don't expect to be asked."

There's a second piece as well. Powell works hard to make sure that the individual who takes initiative doesn't get scapegoated if things go wrong. He tries to understand what happened, learn whatever lessons are available to be learned, and move on. "If you screw up, just vow to do better next time," he told members of his battalion. "I don't hold grudges. I don't keep book."

So what's happened at FBO? Good things, it seems. Charles Williams has challenged his unit to adopt private-sector real estate practices, and his team has evidently embraced the assignment. "Everything we do here," he says, "will have to pass a business test." Echoing Powell's core belief about performance, Williams asserts that his will be a results-based organization. It remains to be seen, of course, what will happen if and when something goes wrong. But so far, avoiding no's has served Williams and his organization well.

Sometimes, of course, the "no" is difficult or impossible to avoid. Sometimes there's a specific door that has to be opened, or a specific hurdle that needs to be overcome, or a specific sanction that has to be removed—and when the answer is no, that may be the end of the story. But sometimes no isn't really no, but only "sort of no." Powell's career suggests that it is sometimes worth testing the no that has already landed on your desk.

For example, as a young soldier, Powell spoke to his assignment officer at the end of his time at Leavenworth about his [Powell's] interest in attending graduate school. The assignment officer took one look at Powell's grades and told the ambitious young soldier that he wasn't graduate school material. It sounded like a pretty solid no.

Powell, although still young, was already wise to the wiring of the bureaucracy. He told the assignment officer that, graduate school material or not, he was planning to apply. Therefore, he said, he would need it *in writing* that he wasn't allowed to apply. The "sort of no" went away, and Powell went off to graduate school.

STRETCHING THE ENVELOPE CAN BOOST MORALE

What is stretching, pushing, being proactive, and dodging no's all about? Ultimately, it's all about the *individual spirit*. It's about what makes a job worth doing and, to some extent, what makes life worth living.

In one interview, Powell was asked if his remarkable career could be attributed to some "grand scheme." No, he replied, there wasn't a grand scheme. "I set out to be the best soldier I could be," he said. "Everything else followed from that." A simple concept, from an individual who values simplicity—but also a powerful one. Powell has made this and similar statements wherever there's a group willing to listen to him, from adult officers in the military to minority kids involved in his America's Promise foundation:

> **Freedom to be your best means nothing**
> **unless you're willing to do your best.**

How does this fit within the ideas presented in this chapter? I think it's at the core of those ideas. Doing your best is more than just passively waiting for initiatives to come from somewhere else. It's more than just passively waiting for someone else to determine your fate. In most cases, we don't come *near* to doing our best until we tackle things that we might not get away with.

Of course, career skeptics will sneer at this entire discussion, even as they complain about injustices in the organization, the stagnation of their careers, and that "it's impossible to make any change around here, so why even try?" Powell's philosophy is the antidote to this malaise, but one has to have the spirit to embrace it.

Ted Strickler did.

Strickler, the head of the State Department's Office of Foreign Missions, has attained near-legendary status within the department. Prior to Powell's arrival at State, Strickler fought tenaciously to accomplish something that might seem faintly ridiculous to individuals outside of government life. For *two full years*, he attempted to get the department to drop the requirement that overseas correspondence had to be attached to a legal-sized ($8\frac{1}{2}$" x 14") cover sheet. Strickler argued, time and time again, that it would be far more cost- and time-efficient to use $8\frac{1}{2}$" x 11" paper.

The good news is that Strickler ultimately won his battle, and the policy was changed. Strickler was so frustrated with the change process, however, that he organized a campaign that he called "SOS for DOS." Prior to the 2000 presidential election, without asking anybody's permission, the group garnered more than 1,600 signatures worldwide on a letter asking the next secretary of state to provide the "support, involvement and leadership needed to undertake a long-term, nonpartisan effort to modernize and strengthen the Department of State."

No doubt some incoming secretaries of state, newly installed in office, would have avoided this kind of trouble-maker like the plague. Powell took the opposite approach. He invited Strickler and his colleagues in for a meeting, accepted their petitions, and told them that he would welcome their help in promoting significant change within the Department of State. "We came away very encouraged," announced a somewhat surprised Strickler after the meeting.

A skeptic might well ask, "But suppose Strickler had failed or suppose the next secretary of state didn't take kindly to internal agitators?" Those are fair questions. But it is worth pointing out that he *didn't* fail. He pushed, stretched the envelope, stepped outside the confines of the playbook, changed a silly policy, and picked the right moment to make his move with his incoming superior. And because the incoming leader was Powell, all this agitation fell on welcoming ears. Strickler's stature—and, presumably, his career prospects—was considerably enhanced. And because Powell supported Strickler, a budding "let's try it" culture was reinforced in the State Department.

The point of this discussion is that regardless of where they sit in the hierarchy, good leaders aren't reckless—*but*— they don't wait for official blessing to push the envelope either.

Middle managers who wait for top management to "get religion" and officially bless all initiatives will be waiting a long time. Katherine D'Urso, a director at Coopers & Lybrand, is pretty blunt in her assessment: "Supplicants don't get respect. At best, they get pity. Usually they get ignored....Whether you work in a 16,000-person firm like Coopers & Lybrand or a 50-person startup, the only way you'll change things is by working to change them."

Yes, courage is involved in this process. Leadership demands courage, especially when it pertains to change that makes a difference. Living the lessons in this chapter will boost the prospects of both your organization and your career.

And, by the way, if your organization relentlessly smothers your efforts to initiate positive change, then you're probably on a sinking ship anyway. In that case, do what a lot of good players do: Polish your résumé and look for the first opportunity to get out. Remember that you'll be a lot more marketable to another organization if you can point to a significant change program you championed than if you simply say you took orders well.

SUMMARY

You don't know what you can get away with until you try. So try. Yes, some initiatives may require upper management approval, especially if they involve big capital expenditures. When the time comes, go for the yes—push, and push hard.

But unless you're a member of senior management, initiatives that require huge budget allocations are the exceptions to the rule anyway. Most worthy initiatives don't wind up turning the entire organization inside out. So (within reason) as long as you're honestly trying to improve things and achieve the organization's goals, don't demand a formal blessing from the people upstairs. Do your homework. Partner with others who feel the same way. Strike the elusive balance between prudently picking your battles (good) and timidly playing it safe (bad). Then make your move. Remember: Your first name doesn't have to be "president" or "CEO" in order for you to be a leader.

If you're challenged along the way, *fight* for your cause. Explain your actions by invoking both organizational aspirations and sound business principles. Make sure, too, that you're delivering convincing *results*. If Powell were your boss, he'd be looking for evidence of positive impact.

Does this involve personal risk? Yes, in many (maybe even most) circumstances. But given the realities that organizations in both the private and public sector are now facing, there's greater peril—both personal and organizational—in playing it safe. A few years ago, one successful manager explained his rationale for all his "don't ask" initiatives: "Yes, there is a risk in doing this," he told me. "There is a bigger risk in not doing this." Moral of the story once again: Regardless of your position, don't play it safe.

POWELL PRINCIPLES

1. **Live the old military adage: "No guts, no glory."** You are likely to accomplish more by taking calculated, intelligent risks than if you play it safe. It is easier to get forgiveness than permission, particularly in these complex times.

2. **Do your best by pursuing every avenue.** Pushing the envelope means leaving nothing on the table, so to speak. Many a career has been stymied because of a manager's unwillingness to take things to the next level. It is often

success on that next level that separates the highly valued employee from the also-ran.

3. **Make everybody want to stretch.** Whether you lead a small department or a large organization, it's up to you to create a context in which everyone wants to take actions that make a difference.

4. **Don't punish for failure.** As long as people are not subjecting your organization to undue risk, *it's never a sin to fail* when pursuing a good objective using sensible tools and tactics. Find ways to keep the organization from making the same mistake twice.

5. **Don't invest in organizations that punish risk takers.** This is the employee's corollary of principle 3. If you work for an organization that smothers change efforts and punishes risk takers, start working on your exit strategy. Remember: You're much more attractive to prospective employers if you can point to a significant change program that you personally championed.

CHAPTER 5

THE CHIEF "DIS-ORGANIZER"

"Keep looking below surface appearances.
Don't shrink from doing so just
because you might not
like what you find."

ONE REASON WHY Colin Powell is an effective leader is that he is not easily misled by superficial analyses, surface truths, or "spin." In fact, this is a trait that is shared by every good leader that I've come across. They're experienced. They're hard to snow, snooker, or hoodwink. They know that the best paint job can be used to hide nasty things beneath the surface.

At the same time, they're hard to stampede. They've seen lots of dire predictions turn out to be Chicken Little warnings: The sky is falling! Very often, as it turns out, the sky isn't falling.

One way in which effective leaders guard against surprises, as Powell suggests, is through a more or less relentless process of digging and probing, combined with a clear and unblinking eye. If they dig and find a mess, well, they acknowledge that it's a mess, and they take steps to clean it up. If they dig and find a hidden diamond, they celebrate—and then, of course, they keep digging.

It was Powell's many years in the military, with its often Byzantine structures and processes, that taught him these valuable leadership lessons. For example, during his command in Gelnhausen, Germany, in the late 1950s, Powell began focusing on some confusing signals that were coming out of the Army's local equipment maintenance system. Gradually, he came to understand what was going on.

The system was so convoluted that nobody could figure out how to actually make it work. So instead of demanding improvements to the system, the soldiers simply went to the local junkyard to procure the spare parts that they needed. Then—and here comes the really bad part, organizationally speaking—they would concoct the necessary paperwork to make it look as if they had followed procedure, thereby concealing the shortcomings of the maintenance system. Even though he was "in charge," it was very difficult for Powell to see through the deception to the reality.

In Germany, this corrupt system was mostly an annoyance. But the emergence of what Powell called a "cover-it-up mindset" was a pernicious and troubling development throughout the U.S. military. As Powell saw it, this institutionalized mindset seriously hampered the armed forces' ability to carry out their mission in the Vietnam conflict.

And Vietnam provided plenty of additional examples of wishful thinking and obscured vision. Like many others who fought in Vietnam, Powell found himself increasingly dismayed at the widening gulf between the reality of the Vietnamese conflict and the government's perception (or depiction) of that reality. As early as 1963, seemingly authoritative government analyses "proved" that the United States and its allies were winning the war, but nothing that Powell or the other soldiers on the front lines were experiencing supported this optimistic viewpoint. The nation's leaders, it seemed, either weren't seeing what was going on or didn't understand what they were seeing. In either case, this was a failure of leadership.

SUCCESS OFTEN BREEDS FAILURE

Why can't some leaders see straight, or think straight? Perversely, they may be blinded by their own success. In fact, I've found that one of the best predictors of an organization's future failure is its success today. Why? Because all too often, success breeds complacency. "Look at our victories," says the complacent leader. "Look at our hardware, our manpower, our returns, our balance sheet, and our press clippings. We're doing just fine. Why change anything?"

In today's turbulent environment, such thinking is downright dangerous. Complacency is an organizational virus. Left unchecked, it gradually immobilizes people. And when it morphs into more deadly strains like delusion (as in, "the good times will never end!") or arrogance (as in, "we're invincible!"), then the hard fall is probably just around the corner.

Effective leaders nip complacency in the bud, and feel great urgency about doing so. As Bob Ulrich, chairman of the retailing giant Target, wrote me, "Along with leaders in every other industry, we are susceptible to complacency and must root out routineness every day." In fact, effective leaders often push themselves to the other end of the spectrum—that is, away from complacency and toward paranoia. "Only the paranoid survive," as Intel's Andy Grove likes to put it. Effective leaders fight the complacency virus *personally* and *urgently*.

How is this accomplished? Powell has already given us a good answer: "Keep looking below surface appearances. Don't shrink from doing so just because you might not like what you find." Effective leaders *find the truth and face the truth*. They use the truth to make decisions that will move their organizations forward.

In many cases where an organization's vulnerabilities are lurking below the surface (like Powell's maintenance system in Germany), change is resisted by people at every level. Very often, in such circumstances, someone delivers the classic line of procrastination: "If it ain't broke, don't fix it." But again, this is the slogan of people who are complacent, arrogant, or scared. It reflects a mindset that assumes that tomorrow will grow out of today in a tidy and linear fashion. But as we've seen in prior chapters, life is rarely tidy or linear. If you survey a complex organization and conclude that nothing is broken, you haven't looked hard enough.

Leaders need to look hard. They need to look beneath the surface. When Powell took charge in West Germany, he assumed command of a corps that was stationed in ten separate communities. He put out the word to his commanders in those communities that they'd have plenty of notice before his first visit. Subsequently, though, they'd get very little notice that the boss was on his way—"just enough time to let you get the coffee table dusted and the underwear picked up," as he put it. His point was not to trip anyone up, but to get a look at reality with the least possible varnish on it. It was, he said, the only way he could learn what was really going on in the organization for which he was responsible. He understood that a periodic, well-publicized regal visit to the field would be unlikely to get him below the surface.

Think of all the forces that work against someone like Powell getting an unvarnished look at *anything*. We've talked about the power of the status quo: *I like my current setup, and I don't want you changing it.* In almost any complex human organization, moreover, there are at least a few people who've got something hidden under the rug that they don't want the boss getting a good look at—whether it's a sin of omission or a sin of commission. And in many cases, the boss, too, may have ample reason to squint at reality. After all, didn't a lot of these beneath-the-surface problems take root on his or her watch? If so, then the boss will have to own up to some mistakes and make some jarring changes.

That's when the defenders of the status quo get mobilized, of course. That's when all forces converge to stop change. But there really is no alternative to change under such circumstances. The organization can't *survive*, let alone thrive, without change that is grounded in data and intuition. The leader must ferret out reality before it's too late to embrace the right course of action.

DON'T TAKE ALL THE PEOPLE AT THEIR WORD

One measure of an effective leader is the "gut check." The effective leader looks hard at the evidence that's being presented by the people under his or her command, and runs a gut check: *I know what I'm supposed to feel about this. Now, how do I really feel about this? Do I believe this reality?*

In October 1978, then-Colonel Powell flew to Iran's capital, Teheran, to check out how things were going with our then-ally, Shah Mohammed Reza Pahlavi. There had been rumblings in the intelligence community that Muslim fundamentalists might make a move to overthrow the Shah's regime. Their spiritual leader, Ayatollah Khomeini, was then living in exile in Paris and was regularly calling upon the faithful to rise up against the Shah. But could an aging religious leader thousands of miles from home really constitute a threat to the Peacock Throne?

In Iran, Powell was treated to an elaborate military pageant, designed to convince him that the Shah's regime was invulnerable. There were lavish dinners, endless parades, and impressive air shows. He reviewed the entire array of military hardware that the United States had provided Iran, including F-14s, then the deadliest fighter plane in the world. He heard reassurances from all quarters that the impeccably dressed "Immortals" (the Shah's crack troops) would fight forever to protect their leaders. He was told that the Iranian people, including the lower-class *homofars* in the Iranian military, fully supported the regime.

Powell reviewed all this evidence, and decided that something was amiss. What about those street skirmishes between fundamentalist mobs and the police (which the authorities were quick to explain away)? And what about the American Air Force captain who had confided to Powell that he personally wouldn't count on either the battle readiness of the fighter pilots (mostly members of the privileged upper classes) or the loyalty of the *homofar* personnel who maintained the powerful F-14s? When the pageantry was over and Powell had time to gather his thoughts during the long flight home, he found himself wondering whether he had seen the real Iran, or only a shell that had been specially prepared to conceal reality.

Three months later, he got his answer. The masses rose up in the name of the Ayatollah. The Immortals, as Powell later wrote, "cracked like a crystal goblet" on the first day of fighting. The *homofars* in the Iranian Air Force immediately threw in their lot with the revolutionaries. The Peacock Throne collapsed, the Shah went into a humiliating exile, and the generals who had hosted Colonel Powell were summarily executed.

In the end, Powell reflected, "all our investment...came to naught. When the Shah fell, our Iran policy fell with him. All the billions we had spent there only exacerbated conditions, and contributed to the rise of a fundamentalist regime implacably opposed to us to this day."

Where was the failure of leadership? Certainly in Iran, where an arrogant autocrat allowed himself to get terminally out of touch with the people he was allegedly leading. And just as certainly in the United States, where several generations of policy makers, eager to perceive a solid ally in a region of the world where America had few friends, simply refused to see the situation for what it was. Colonel Powell's misgivings notwithstanding, they saw what they wanted to see until it was far too late to stay ahead of change.

BECOMING A "DIS-ORGANIZER"

So, what's the prescription that grows out of these observations? The job of the leader is not to be the chief organizer, but to be the chief *dis-organizer*. A dis-organizer is someone who continually picks at and harasses the routine of the organization. A dis-organizer lifts up the covers, looks under the bed, and runs a finger along the tops of the bookcases, all so that he or she can pose and begin to answer the key question: What are we doing, right or wrong, and how can it be improved?

When a leader asks, "Why do we need four expensive, time-consuming sign-off steps for a simple requisition?" he's being a dis-organizer. When he offers a "why not?" alternative like, "Why not provide computer network skills for front-line people so they can make those decisions themselves?" he's being a dis-organizer.

When a leader asks, "Why do we need this monthly in-house meeting at all?" she's being a dis-organizer. When she offers a "why not?" alternative like "Why don't the appropriate people simply meet on the supplier site until this problem is solved?" she's being a dis-organizer.

I've already described Powell's dis-organizing activities when he took over as chairman of the Joint Chiefs of Staff. In the early 1990s, the American military was generally regarded as a highly effective fighting force. (The Gulf War would soon reinforce that image.) But Powell chose to look more closely at the situation.

He listened carefully to intelligence estimates, computer projections, and other "expert advice" from the usual sources, and then he tested those data against his own experience and knowledge. He made a series of projections (startlingly accurate, as it turned out) about where the armed forces would be needed in the next decade, and where they would not. Then, to the dismay of many both inside and outside the services, he acted on his conclusions, reducing personnel and resources by significant amounts. The result was a military machine that was both more efficient, more nimble, and more appropriate to the (relatively) peaceful decade of the 1990s.

To be a dis-organizer, a leader must be uneasy with routine and habit, vigilant against complacency, and ruthless in attacking smugness and arrogance. To be a dis-organizer, a leader must be restless and curious. He must continually doubt, question, and challenge. She must continually solicit and develop alternatives and chart better paths. A dis-organizing leader becomes an *agent provocateur*, an old French espionage term that translates as a "provocative change agent."

Dis-organizing is so important for competitive success that good leaders must inspire this same disruptive habit in others. I believe that any blueprint for leadership ought to include the following principle: *Explain to your employees why you're digging beneath the surface, and make it clear why they need to be doing it, too.*

This is in large part a process of education. It's unrealistic to expect people to make big changes strictly on faith, or in response to preaching or pontificating. Figure out what troubled your gut in the first place, and *share* it with them. Show them the data and the trends about bureaucracy, customers, competitors, new technologies, or whatever it is that's failing your gut check. Discuss threats and opportunities to the enterprise. Cite real events in the recent history of your organization—like a big quality problem or a major customer defection—to frame the learning points and determine future actions. Hammer away at both the negative and the positive: Ignoring this stuff can be lethal, and dealing with it can be rejuvenating.

TRUTH PAYS DIVIDENDS

Digging is hard work, especially when the soil is rocky and resistant. However, if it leads to truth, that's good for both the organization and the individual. Why is it so important for leaders to get beneath the surface and constantly monitor the environments in which they operate? There are at least two compelling reasons, one individual and the other organizational. Let's look at the individual first. As consultant and ex-IBMer Dan Sweeney told me, "Change makes us reorder priorities and do a lot of *work*—work which we didn't expect to have to do. It makes our past decisions wrong, so we have to make new ones. It makes our plans wrong, so we have to make new ones. It makes our goals and aspirations wrong, so we have to make new ones. Change makes us reorder priorities and do all this additional work."

In the short run, that's an unpleasant prospect for many. For leaders who follow Powell's advice, however, this work is not something to be avoided. Why? Because the work that goes on beneath the surface is often unpredictable, stimulating, and exciting. And by definition, it is work that is absolutely vital to the long-term health of the organization. (You wouldn't be dis-organizing for anything less.) So it's highly gratifying work. It's work that recharges your psychic batteries, rather than draining them.

We've already talked about the compelling organizational reasons to be a pest. Let's face it, for all the noisy chatter in today's business press about the importance and inevitability of change, many of the things we are expected to do in organizations confound innovation. Our planning processes assume linearity and make us hate surprises. (Surprises are nonlinear.) When we spend all that time and money coming up with a plan, we have all kinds of incentives to stick with that plan. Budgetary surprises make us look like bad managers. Disruptions, even demonstrably creative ones, are looked at askance.

So we start papering over the gulfs that emerge between plan and reality. Rather than adjusting to a reality that we couldn't have anticipated, we try to bend reality so that it conforms to our expensive and ornate plan. We stop doing the real work, and instead concentrate on spinning. Gradually, we find ourselves living in and defending a spin culture—that is, the opposite of a truth culture.

You may recall that, in 1983, Soviet fighter pilots shot down a commercial Korean Air Lines jet that had accidentally drifted into Soviet airspace. In the aftermath of this tragedy, Powell recalls that he was taken aback by the wave of excuses, blaming-the-victim stories (the jet was a "spy plane"), and rationalizations that emerged from the Soviet government.

It was as if the entire governmental apparatus, corrupted by years of spinning and dissembling, was constitutionally unable to either see or tell the truth. This was all the more bizarre because it was clear that *the truth was going to come out.* No matter how the Soviets spun the story, the serious problems of communication and discipline that were then plaguing their military infrastructure were going to emerge. All the energy that they were putting into spin could have been better used to improve the organization.

> *It is best to get the facts out*
> *as soon as possible, even when*
> *new facts contradict the old.*

So don't waste energy torturing the truth. Don't waste energy trying to make reality conform to the company line. Don't take pride in crafting what Powell calls the "smooth lie."

> *Untidy truth is better than*
> *smooth lies that unravel*
> *in the end anyway.*

Focus on truth telling. Tell it like it is. In cooperation with others above and below you in the hierarchy, look for real solutions to your organization's real problems. Don't call half a loaf a loaf.

> *I have not allowed myself to be coerced...*
> *to provide very, very cheap [solutions]*
> *that look neat but won't accomplish*
> *the intended purpose.*

ASK THE TOUGHEST,
MOST UNCOMFORTABLE QUESTIONS

I was nearing completion of this book when, in the fall of 2001, the United States was subjected to terrorist bombings and subsequent outrages. The nation was frightened, frustrated, and of course plunged into mourning. Thousands of lives were lost, and enormous sums of money had to go into the rebuilding effort. By almost any measure, it was a disaster.

But as many observers noted, that disaster forced Americans (policymakers and private citizens alike) to embark on a search for truth. We began asking ourselves uncomfortable, dis-organizing questions. When the Soviet Union collapsed a decade ago, for example, did we become complacent? Were we mesmerized by the surface appearance that all was well—politically, militarily, and economically? Did we allow our intelligence mechanisms to atrophy? How could we have missed the fact (so obvious in retrospect) that there were people out there who truly hated us, and who were organizing clandestinely—even within our own borders—to inflict grievous harm on us?

Questions like these inevitably lead to untidy truths. They are painful to ask and painful to answer. And yet they constitute the unavoidable first step toward renewal. They blow away "spin" like so much chaff and prepare the ground for real change. As President Bush stated in a powerful address to a joint session of Congress, "Great harm has been done to us. We have suffered great loss. And in our grief and anger, we have found our mission and our moment."

In the business world, of course, the stakes aren't so high. But they're high enough—especially for the individuals who are responsible for charting an organization's course and future. The quest for mission and moment can grow out of a catastrophe, or, far better, it can grow out of a culture of relentless probing. A culture of probing, truth telling, and dis-organizing discovers the catastrophe before it happens. And, more positively, it unearths lucrative new opportunities: new niches, new products, new relationships, new services. Historically, some of the most impressive commercial and brand breakthroughs (think Schwab, FedEx, Wal-Mart, CNN, Body Shop, Nokia, Palm, Nike, AOL Time Warner, and many others) were driven by leaders who were tenaciously prepared to break through the surface of conventional wisdom in the industry—who were, in a word, dis-organizers.

SUMMARY

Effective leaders understand the importance of rejecting the superficial and embracing the underlying realities. This is a key success ingredient. Only by delving below the surface will leaders be able to discern the truth and shape an organizational plan based on the new realities.

An unwillingness to face up to reality and an eagerness to protect the status quo are usually reflections of complacency. Complacency is the enemy of growth. The best leaders fight complacency. They are "dis-organizers"—individuals who are not afraid to shake things up and find a better way of doing things.

According to Powell, leaders ask, "What needs to be done?" Then they follow up with a second question: "What can and should I do to make a difference?" And these are the questions that compel people to *look below the surface*. They are questions that reflect responsibility, integrity, and—ultimately—leadership.

POWELL PRINCIPLES

1. **Be a "dis-organizer."** Wage war on smugness and arrogance. Never stop doubting and challenging. Challenge habits and conventional wisdom. Always look for a better way to develop alternative and better paths. Be the organization's primary agent for change.

2. **Don't accept things at face value.** Don't fall prey to the alluring descriptions of the Peacock Throne. Maintain a healthy dose of skepticism. Often, things are not as they appear. Do a gut check. Always dig beneath the surface.

3. **Remember that success can breed failure, and that complacency is the enemy.** In today's world, contentment with the status quo is dangerous. Lead with a healthy dose of paranoia.

4. **Put truth and integrity above all else.** Remember Powell's wisdom: "Untidy truth is better than smooth lies that unravel in the end anyway." Don't be afraid to confront or tell "untidy truth."

5. **Dig, dig, and dig some more.** An open-door policy is a good thing. But it alone (or even in combination with state visits to the field) won't get you to the truth below the surface. It is the leader's responsibility to constantly and proactively probe below the surface.

CHAPTER 6

WHEN TO CHALLENGE THE PROS

"Every organization should
tolerate rebels who tell
the emperor he has no clothes."

THIS POWELL LESSON is likely to make some readers nervous. It's about *challenging the authorities*—maybe even including your own boss. But those who want to have a significant impact on their organizations can't duck this responsibility. Powell's advice on this subject is succinct, and has profound implications for managers and professionals at every level: "*Don't be afraid to challenge the pros, even in their own backyard.*"

Who are the "pros"? Simply put, they're the people with authority and status. Most of them are inside the organization: your peers, your colleagues, your bosses, your boss's bosses, and so on. They run the place, wielding either formal or implicit power. But they may also be outside the organization—consultants, accountants, lawyers, or other providers of professional services. Or they may straddle some sort of divide, such as a major shareholder. The one thing they all have in common is that they are able to wield significant power.

Some pros have earned their positions of power through exceptional performance, by acquiring and exercising vital skills. Others have earned their power position mainly by kissing up to the right people, by skillfully expropriating the work of others, or simply by staying out of the way of trouble. I'd call these characters "phony pros," but in many cases their clout is no less real.

Because pros have clout, they can steer the enterprise in the right direction or, just as easily, down an errant path. They can make things happen or stop things from happening. They can raise spirits or depress them. They can affect people's performance in either positive or negative ways. In extreme cases, they can put the organization, or people within it, in danger.

This lesson was once forced upon Powell in an unusual setting: in a "Bird Dog" jet high above the troubled plains of Vietnam. Powell had been assigned to command the Hue Citadel airfield. He was an unusual choice, since airfields were almost always run by Air Force officers, rather than by a member of the Army brass like Powell. The Air Force flyboys seemed to resent the choice, and one pilot (a pro, in the lingo of this chapter) decided to show Powell which branch of the service was the boss of the skies. He took Powell on a wild high-speed flight, complete with rolls, dives, and other stomach-turning stunts. Apparently, Powell bore up reasonably well under this high-altitude hazing.

Then, looking out the window, Powell thought he noticed unfamiliar terrain below. No, said the pilot, he knew exactly where they were, and they were above safe territory. The pro had spoken authoritatively, but Powell immediately challenged him. In polite but forceful language, he ordered the pilot to turn the plane around and *get them out of there*. As it later turned out, the plane had been flying over enemy territory, thereby exposing both it and its occupants to unnecessary risk.

The incident resembles a number of others in Powell's career. In all cases, he treats the people around him, including the pros, with respect. He affords them their dignity. But he is fully prepared to assert that the pros can be wrong—that they can make ill-advised decisions, act inappropriately, or inadvertently give bad advice. When that happens, he pushes back and challenges them. In fact, he believes that everyone in an organization has an *obligation* to pose this kind of challenge—not only peer-to-peer and down the ladder, but also up the ladder.

Obviously, this philosophy won't work in a hierarchy that takes every "up-the-ladder" challenge as an act of insubordination. (Organizations that shoot the messenger stop getting messages.) So one of Powell's principles states that "every organization should tolerate rebels who tell the emperor he has no clothes."

In fact, Powell personalizes this philosophy. As he tells his people:

> **This particular emperor expects
> to be told when he is naked.**

Not all organizations have the benefit of a leader who asks to be told when he's naked. But most organizations (even the most buttoned-down, hierarchical ones) usually have some channel for funneling bad news to the emperor. Or, looking at the same issue from another angle, most organizations have at least a few people who get away with being rebels. Usually, these are people who have found a way to deliver bad news appropriately: with civility, sound research, good timing, a dose of humor, or whatever. But don't use the lack of these role models as an excuse not to act. You *have* to act, says Powell; you have to challenge the pros.

THE GHOSTS OF VIETNAM

To understand the origins of Powell's philosophy on personal responsibility and challenging the pros, we must look once again at his experiences during the Vietnam War era. In his memoir, Powell described a painful lesson that he, along with many of his colleagues in the officer corps, learned during that period. He described what he called "a policy that had become bankrupt." The leaders in the field kept up the charade, never telling the secretary of state or the president that this was a war that was not being won.

Powell and many of his fellow junior officers vowed that when they were senior enough to call the shots, they would not make the same mistake. They would speak up. And, just as important, they would listen when they were approached by earnest young men and women with an urge to talk to the emperor.

Fast forward to 1990, when Powell's moment had arrived. He had four stars on his shoulder, he was chairman of the Joint Chiefs of Staff, and he had the ear of the most powerful civilian leaders in the country. In that role, as he later related in a joint interview with PBS and BBC, he attended a critical August 3 National Security Council meeting with the senior President George Bush, Defense Secretary Dick Cheney, and other senior members of the government. The purpose of the meeting was to determine the appropriate U.S. response to Iraq's invasion of Kuwait. Powell, thinking that he was hearing muddled thinking, started playing a role that PBS/BBC later described as "party pooper." As Powell put it:

*The key decision that came out of that meeting
is...we will defend Saudi Arabia. There was no
debate about that. The question I then posed
was, 'Then what? Should we be prepared to go
forward and fight for Kuwait, to eject the Iraqi
army out of Kuwait to do what?' And I guess
some people suggested that that was not the
correct thing for me to ask, but I asked it.*

Later on in that same meeting, Powell asked what he sub-sequently called the "draw a line in the sand" question. He asked bluntly if America was prepared "to draw a line in the sand now. Does everybody agree it's worth going to war to reverse the invasion of Kuwait?"

As he later recalled, "that was not a well received state-ment." In fact, Cheney chided Powell rather bluntly later that day, reminding him that his job was only to provide military options, not to act as secretary of state. Powell came back at him with yet another challenge: "I will do military options.... But it is important that we start off with a common under-standing of what it is we are trying to achieve."

Why was Powell a pro-challenger and a party pooper? Because he was uncomfortable with the possibility that the individuals in the room would be content to leave the U.S. mission ambiguous. He had been there before, and he had seen the disasters that ensued. As he explains it:

*Perhaps I was the ghost of Vietnam.... There
had been cases in our past...when senior
leaders, military leaders did not force civilians
to make those kind of clear choices, and if it
caused me to be the skunk at the picnic...
(Powell sniffs), take a deep breath.*

COURAGE: A HALLMARK OF LEADERSHIP

Challenging the pros takes guts. But standing by one's convictions is a hallmark of leadership. And if one looks carefully at how a pro gets to be a pro, it turns out that there are solid reasons to challenge the pros, even on their own home court. Most likely, these individuals achieved their status through past struggles and solid accomplishments. Once their value to the organization became clear (once their skills and wisdom were understood for what they were), they began to be called upon in times of crisis.

But those skills can become outdated in turbulent environments and times of flux. And even if that's not the case, we've seen in Chapter 2 that all organizations benefit from a 'clash of ideas.' Either way, challenging the pros can revitalize an organization. Fresh ideas, insights, and initiatives, especially those that are informed by recent experiences in the trenches, are vital. The troops have a responsibility to come forward with those ideas—and their leaders have a responsibility to listen, sift and sort, and move the best ideas up the ladder—even if that means butting heads with those in charge.

Sometimes I give speeches to corporate groups that incorporate some of these ideas. And not uncommonly, after such a presentation, some earnest person in what turns out to be a middle-management position approaches me with a mix of enthusiasm and frustration. "Gee," he or she finally blurts out, "I wish my *boss* could have heard you. We're going down the wrong path, for sure. But what can *I* do?"

My response is usually something along the lines of, "Don't be afraid to challenge the higher-ups." And sometimes I can see, in the eyes of these frustrated middle managers, that they think I am being naïve. (Sometimes they come right out and *tell* me that I'm being naïve.) When that happens, I sometimes relate the story of Barry Rand, who until a few years ago was a senior executive with Xerox. "If you have a yes-man or yes-woman working for you," he used to tell his management team, "then one of you is redundant."

Wouldn't you expect the military to be the last place that you could get away with being a rebel or a naysayer? And yet Powell as a military man regularly took on his superiors. For example, as a brigadier general with the Fourth Infantry Division in Fort Carson, Colorado, Powell found an atmosphere in which morale was sagging and negative pressures were seriously hurting the division. Against the advice of others in the division, Powell decided to discuss the situation with the general in charge, a man who was legendary for not taking criticism (or judging critics) favorably. Powell knew that his suggestions might be misconstrued, and that his own career might suffer for his decision to challenge the pros. But he felt strongly that his position as assistant division commander required him to look after the interests of his division in this way.

As it turned out, Powell had good reason to have been concerned. The general, who before this encounter had been very happy with Powell's style of leadership, now set out to sabotage his [Powell's] career. The general wrote an efficiency report that essentially damned Powell with faint praise. In the extremely competitive world of the Army, a one-star general with only a ho-hum efficiency report could not hope for a promotion—and without a promotion, his military career would effectively be over. Powell dusted off his résumé and started thinking about the next (nonmilitary) phase of his life.

In the end, of course, Powell's job-hunting phase proved short lived. The head of Forces Command (FORSCOM), General Richard G. Cavazos, had observed Powell's superior in action, and had a clearer grasp of the situation than Powell suspected. In fact, Cavazos had been in a meeting with Powell and the offended commanding general, and he had been impressed with Powell's willingness to stand up for his division. Without fanfare, Powell was put back on the military fast track, and the lackluster efficiency report was filed away and forgotten.

This lesson appears to have had a profound impact on Powell. He evidently resolved to always speak his mind, even if some of those around him would have preferred a silent follower. During the administration of the senior President Bush, Powell got a reputation for asking the local pros—that is, his superiors in the cabinet—lots of annoying questions. "I have been repeatedly criticized for always asking these questions," he recalls, so much so that on more than one occasion, he was taken "out to the woodshed" for some discipline. But again, this degree of candor didn't hurt his reputation within the Bush administration, nor (as later events clearly showed) did it hurt his subsequent career.

DIVIDENDS IN DEFYING

Good leaders are frequently taken to the woodshed for challenging the process. Even today, Powell is not immune from the heat. The September 10, 2001, issue of *Time* magazine featured a critical cover story on Secretary of State Powell. It pointed to the existence of friction within the Bush team—a friction that sometimes left Powell as the "odd man out."

Time's assessment boiled down to this: "The differences within the [Bush] team are not about goals so much as about the manner of accomplishing them. Powell is a multilateralist; other Bush advisors are unilateralists. He's internationalist; they're America first." Powell's belief, said *Time*, is that America can best lead "not by using our strength and position of power to get back behind our walls, but by being engaged in the world."

I won't venture an opinion as to whether Powell was "right" or "wrong" in his position. I cite the *Time* article merely to underscore the discomfort that is likely to be inherent in challenging the pros—especially if one is going up against smart, tough individuals like Vice President Dick Cheney and Defense Secretary Don Rumsfeld, not to mention their capable, like-minded allies such as Condoleezza Rice and Paul Wolfowitz. Powell, always the gentleman, summarized his situation with apparent understatement: "Sometimes I get frustrated making the case that the U.S. is not unilateralist."

Of course, very shortly after that particular issue of *Time* hit the stands, the World Trade Center and Pentagon attacks stunned the civilized world—and forced the Bush administration to examine its most fundamental assumptions. Suddenly, Powell's steady drumbeat that "the world is too complicated for anyone to be unilateralist" had gained enormous credibility. The Bush team set out to create a coalition among nations that it had previously chosen to ignore, in an effort to find and fight an enemy that apparently has a presence in more than sixty countries. Simultaneously, the team began to aggressively pursue diplomatic and economic pressure in conjunction with military responses. Even "nation-building" rose in prominence as a viable strategy.

For our discussion, it is not important whether multilateralism or unilateralism has been crowned victorious. True, as the *Economist* points out, the sudden threat to America's security, which one might have expected to strengthen the unilateralists' point of view, "has actually pushed them closer to Mr. Powell." But at the same time, the unilateral/multilateral tension within the Bush administration continues to simmer beneath the surface, although the principal players minimize their differences. Powell, for his part, has said that "within a range, we usually come into agreement." Nevertheless, the *Economist* has observed that "if military action widens, and especially if it brings in Iraq, Mr. Powell may again find himself in the minority."

My point again is not that Powell "won" any ideological war. My point is that his consistency and courage—even when it came to challenging tough, powerful pros—paid off not only in policy but also in his stature and influence. As *Newsweek* observed, "on an organizational level, the still murky war is also being prosecuted with the kind of steely clarity and message control favored by the secretary of state."

The bottom line for leadership is that challenging the pros can yield big payoffs, but it's a demanding exercise that requires courage and persistence. For a true leader, there is no other alternative.

SUMMARY

Powell is very specific that leadership requires "moral, physical, mental, and spiritual courage." Courage is not about self-aggrandizement, bravado, or suicidal initiatives. It's about the willingness to respectfully, relentlessly, and unapologetically challenge people—including the smartest, toughest people around you—in the pursuit of unit goals and performance excellence.

Challenging the pros in their own backyard is not something a leader does as a personal power play or as a "gotcha!" It's done to help the enterprise achieve its mission—which is the first and most important task of leadership.

"I always find it much better to try to solve problems, not create problems for your bosses," Powell says. As noted in Chapter 5, concealing or camouflaging problems doesn't get those problems solved. Those problems have to be brought to the surface, confronted, and wrestled to the ground—which may necessitate challenging some powerful people. That can be uncomfortable for all concerned, but it's what a leader is supposed to do. For Powell, it's not a close call. "I am what I am," he says. "If that sometimes puts me at odds with others, then, well, fine."

So do your homework, get the data, focus on creating value, challenge the process, put your conclusions on the table—and then have the courage and confidence to challenge the pros, even on their own turf. By doing so, you're likely to enhance the value of your organization, help your own career prospects, and be involved in some truly interesting, provocative work.

POWELL PRINCIPLES

1. **Challenge the pros to get to better solutions.** Whether it's you challenging your superiors or your subordinates challenging you, remember that more opinions and more voices usually translates into more alternative options. This is particularly important when events are moving faster than your collective experience has prepared you for.

2. **Emphasize dignity, respect, and honor while disagreeing.** Disagree without being disagreeable. Powell challenges his bosses when necessary, but he does so in a way that respects the dignity of his superiors and preserves the dignity of his own position.

3. **Be patient.** If you're right, the wheel will eventually turn your way. Powell's position as a multilateralist earned him criticism and scorn. But when the pendulum shifted in the wake of the September 2001 terrorist attacks, his views

suddenly came to the fore, because they appeared to be most in touch with a changed world. Sometimes it takes time, and a change of circumstances, before your dissenting opinion can resonate or pay dividends.

5. **Build a setting in which all feel free to speak out.** If you're going to be speaking out, you need to be helping others to speak out, too. (It's the best way to get the best ideas on the table.) Encourage those around you to challenge you and the other senior members of your team.

PART II

POWELL
ON
STRATEGY
AND
EXECUTION

CHAPTER 7

CLOSE WITH
THE ENEMY

*"We had to make sure that we took
the new mission and drove it down to
the last private in the ranks.
Whoever came in and emptied the
trash can at night had to understand the vision."*

WHERE DOES A "mission" come from, and how important is it to the success of a leader?

These are questions that would occur to anyone who was trying to understand the leadership secrets of Colin Powell. But when I met Powell in 2000, he underscored their importance by giving me a photocopy of a single typewritten sheet entitled "The Powell Way." At the bottom of that sheet, which consisted mainly of short bullet points, were some phrases on a topic that I soon learned was near and dear to him:

Mission

- Close with the enemy and destroy him by fire and maneuver
- Reason for existence

As I later learned, Powell first encountered the phrase "close with the enemy" during his Army training at Fort

Benning. Among other things, basic training teaches soldiers that *mission comes first*—closely followed by taking care of the soldiers in your command—and very often, the military mission involves engaging ("closing with") the enemy and destroying it. So almost from his first minutes in uniform, Powell found himself focused on mission. The lesson has stuck with him ever since. For Powell, *mission*—what you're trying to accomplish—is essential to leadership.

But I should make a confession at this point. As I quickly scanned the sheet of paper that Powell handed to me, I decided that he must have made an error. I thought the order of the subheadings should be reversed. Ordinarily, wouldn't one first determine the "reason for existence" (the enterprise's purpose and objective) and *then* aim for the aggressive execution of that mission? Isn't that what good strategy is all about?

Still, I held my tongue. I decided to take the paper home with me and give it more thought. And upon further reflection, I concluded that the order of the bullet points, unconventional as it was in terms of conventional management thinking, was exactly as he had intended.

THE ZEAL TO EXECUTE

Many leaders focus first and foremost on their organization's ideas—its goals, vision, mission statement, and so on. And to be fair, this is a large part of what they're hired and paid to do. Unfortunately, though, many leaders fail to follow through. They consider the implementation of their ideas as a task mostly for other people. (Perhaps some of them think that the sheer power of their ideas will assure success.) *Execution* of the plan becomes an afterthought. And that is why so many grand plans never make it out of the starting gate.

In his tersely worded credo, Powell is telling us something critically important: *Execution matters.* A plan is only as powerful as the *zeal to execute* that lies behind it. Powell believes strongly that there is little sense in even articulating a mission, or laying out a battle plan, unless you are prepared to pursue that mission and fight that battle with complete commitment. In other words, unless you're unequivocally committed to a path, don't even go there. This is why "closing with the enemy" comes first on his list. In wartime, it's what a soldier *must do.*

What I realized, looking at Powell's bullet points, is that their exact sequence is ultimately an arbitrary decision. The fact is, *your purpose must be inseparable from your commitment to achieving it.*

Let's look more closely at that three-word phrase at the bottom of Powell's memo: *reason for existence.* At a fundamental level, the mission ought to be spare, simple, straightforward, and accessible: *Why do we exist? What do we stand for? What exactly are we trying to accomplish? What are we really committed to? How passionate are we about accomplishing it?* This argues for setting aside all the complex plans, algorithms, spreadsheets, and tools of planning—at least for the moment. It calls for a powerful statement of *what we want to achieve* and *how badly we want to get there.*

Part of the goal in mission setting is to generate a powerful internal consensus. *Consensus* has recently acquired a slightly negative connotation, signifying (to some people, at least) that an organization is aiming for the lowest common denominator, and that the result will necessarily be tasteless and odorless. This is unfair. Consider what a lack of consensus means for an organization. Can you really move toward a goal—*any* goal—if there's no agreement on that goal? And the harder the goal, the more commitment and tenacity your organization is going to need. Commitment and tenacity grow, in part, out of consensus.

I've already mentioned the strong influence that Vietnam had on Powell, and the powerful ways in which it shaped his thinking. In that war, the mission was neither understandable nor inspiring. "Containing the spread of communism" and "keeping the dominoes from falling over" were essentially passive, or even negative, goals. As a result, the military lacked purpose and direction.

Because the troops lacked the unifying vision needed to bind them together, there was no consensus, either in Vietnam or on the home front. Accordingly, the effectiveness of the troops was greatly reduced. Racial polarization and drug abuse became serious problems. A new word, "fragging," was invented to describe soldiers killing their own leaders. Over the course of a decade and a half, as the minimal consensus behind our stated goals evaporated, the situation went from bad to worse. "We had entered into a halfhearted half-war," Powell later wrote, "with much of the nation opposed or indifferent, while a small fraction carried the burden."

Powell resolved that this would never happen again. The military would figure out its mission, and then implement the hell out of it. "We had to make sure that we took the new mission," he wrote, "and drove it down to the last private in the ranks. Whoever came in and emptied the trash can at night had to understand the vision." Never again would a soldier—even the one who emptied the trash cans on the graveyard shift—be without a reason for existence.

CLARITY, CONSISTENCY, COMMITMENT

How do we bring this lesson home to a business context? I think Powell is telling us that we must *take on clearly defined battles that can be won, and won decisively.* We must make sure that the goals are understood and endorsed by the people who need to endorse them. (And this ought to be a larger group, rather than a smaller group.) Finally, we need to make it clear that these goals will be pursued with overwhelming strength. All necessary resources will be mobilized to fight our battles and gain our victories.

During the Vietnam conflict, Powell recalls, senior American officials were given to using self-protective phrases and antiseptic metrics (like "option on the table" and "body counts") to paper over the fact that things weren't progressing according to plan. Phrases like these, says Powell, "were fine if beneath them lay a solid mission. But too often these words were used to give the appearance of clarity to mud."

According to Powell, the American intervention in Beirut during the Reagan era suffered from a similar problem. There, Americans entered a situation that "nobody could really quite understand." Instead of becoming clearer and more powerful, the language of leadership became increasingly fuzzy and defensive.

When Powell finally achieved a level of authority where he could influence high-level decision making, he kept these lessons firmly in mind. In the fall of 1989, for example, when the administration of the senior President George Bush was considering action against Panamanian strongman Manuel Noriega, Powell put on the table an absolutely clear mission statement that both reflected what had already been discussed and forced the assembled leaders to make choices. "We take down Noriega, we take the whole Panamanian defense force, and we restore democracy in its totality by putting in a new president and rebuilding the defense force," Powell proposed. "That will solve this problem. That will achieve your political objective in a decisive way."

It was both a synthesis and a challenge. *If you believe what you're saying*, Powell told them, *then here's your mission, and here are your objectives, in clear and compelling language. So, are you willing to commit to them?*

As it turned out, they were, and they did. But a push for clarity and crispness can make the people around you uncomfortable. In fact, this is a constant counterpoint offered by people who have dealt with Powell over the years, and who claim to like and admire him: *If only he didn't feel like he had to push us so hard.* In response, I'm sure, Powell would say that there's no sense in avoiding tough issues, and that there's no honor in hiding behind organizational "mud." Sooner or later, he would say, you'll be forced to speak and act clearly.

THE REAL POWELL DOCTRINE

Powell is sometimes criticized for allegedly being too cautious—for being a "reluctant warrior." But those who follow his thinking about mission understand what lies behind his seeming caution. Powell doesn't lack for courage, nor is there any record of him shying away from a just battle. But the key word here, of course, is *just*. Is the proposed battle tied to a mission, and does that mission command the loyalty of the people who are charged with carrying it out? Powell is simply not interested in saber rattling or other empty gestures that tend to reduce, rather than enhance, a nation's credibility. He's even more wary of knee-jerk "send-in-the-troops" reactions to thorny geopolitical problems: "You do not squander courage and lives without clear purpose," he says, simply, "without the country's backing, and without full commitment.... War is a deadly game and I do not believe in spending the lives of Americans lightly."

Powell recognized the importance of defining a mission and then acting upon it when he was preparing to become a general officer in the late 1960s at Fort Leavenworth. There, Powell not only learned about generalship, but also learned about himself. Looking back years later on his experiences there, Powell explained that he had a tendency to be prudent until he acquired the information he needed. Only then was he ready to move boldly. He knew that his actions and decisions could result in loss of life. But once he decided on a course of action, he struck hard and fast, using all of the power he knew he would need to achieve his mission.

With this context in mind, the now famous "Powell doctrine" becomes perfectly understandable:

> *American military force should only be used in overwhelming strength to achieve well-defined strategic national interests.*

I mentioned earlier that organizations often resort to invoking mud when their mission isn't clear or compelling. This is why Powell is so irritating to some who encounter him. To them, life is too complicated to lend itself to the kind of simplicity that Powell demands. But it's worth reminding ourselves that the Powell doctrine closely tracks the philosophy of Karl von Clausewitz, the brilliant nineteenth-century Prussian military strategist. "No one starts a war, or rather no one in his senses should do so," Clausewitz wrote, "without first being clear in his mind what he intends to achieve by that war and how he intends to achieve it."

In fact, when the twin criteria of the Powell doctrine (clear mission and overwhelming commitment of strength) are satisfied, Powell becomes a very *un*reluctant warrior. At the outset of the Gulf War, for example, he stated at a press briefing that the coalition's strategy for dealing with the Iraqi army was "very, very simple. First, we are going to cut it off, then we are going to kill it." He also wrote to Saddam Hussein that he was perfectly prepared to "destroy the dams on the Tigris and Euphrates rivers and flood Baghdad, with horrendous consequences." These are the words of a leader who knows where he is going, and how he is going to get there.

Leadership is figuring out where you're going, pulling out all the stops, and *never getting distracted*. "Figure out what is crucial," Powell advises, "then stay focused on that. Never allow side issues...to knock you off track." Demonstrate passion, leap over hurdles, see your mission through to the end—and keep a close eye on the language and actions of those around you. When you start hearing fuzzy language and incomplete commitments, take action. "As soon as they tell me [military intervention or humanitarian aid] is limited," Powell has said, "it means they do not care whether you achieve a result or not.... As soon as they tell me 'surgical,' I head for the bunker." There can be no limited commitment.

As of this writing, Colin Powell is at the forefront of an ambitious American effort to destroy global terrorist networks, and he has taken the lead in building a worldwide coalition of partners to achieve that end. It's fair to ask whether the criteria underlying the Powell doctrine have been met. Is the mission clear? Is there a vital national interest? Is there clear support from Congress and the American public? Is the United States prepared to use overwhelming force (military, diplomatic, economic, personal) to achieve its goals? Is the mission achievable? Can we go in, get the job done, and get out again?

The answer to most of these questions is yes. What's not clear, as of this writing, is how and when the mission will end. Ideally, the Powell doctrine contemplates a fast resolution—get in quick and get out quick. (For one thing, it's a lot easier to maintain an unwavering consensus on the mission over a period of weeks or months than over a period of years.)

But Powell has already cautioned us that this particular mission will necessarily be a long-term effort, requiring a sustained commitment over time. "It will not be over," he told the American public, "until we have gotten into the inside of this organization, inside its decision cycle, inside its planning cycle, inside its execution capability, and until we have neutralized and destroyed it. That is our objective." If anything, the likely duration of this mission calls for even more clarity and consistency, and an even higher commitment on the part of our leaders to remind us exactly what we're doing, and why. They will need to reassure us that the objectives are unambiguous and compelling, that there is a clear, sensible plan of action in place, that the right preparation and resources have been brought to bear, and that their foresight has critically addressed the question of what will, and should happen next. As a number of observers have noted, these are the kinds of questions that emerge when one deconstructs the Powell doctrine into a set of practical decision-making tools.

These are also the questions that any leader—in business or government—should regularly confront as top priorities. In my own research, I've found that the best leaders in corporate environments share certain characteristics consistent with the Powell doctrine. They don't blur their company's focus, nor do they waste resources on empty gestures and "sizzle without steak." They pick their battles carefully, choose causes that inspire others, and effectively articulate where they're going and why. They know what purpose they and their teams will commit to without reservation, and they act accordingly. They think big, go for the big win, act decisively with almost ruthless speed and precision, and do not apologize for doing so.

I've also found that leaders who continually reflect on these issues and questions are better able to develop a practical, big-picture vision of the future. Visions based on Powell doctrine considerations have more impact than many traditional "vision statements." The reason is that the latter are often full of glittering generalities and psychobabble, while the former are precise, data-based statements which define the organization's "reason for existence" and commit it to "close with the enemy and destroy him by fire and maneuver." Already, Powell is developing a blueprint of the alliances and global framework that will be necessary to battle world terrorism after the Taliban are neutralized and the current heads of al-Qaeda are dispatched. He is also developing an even bigger picture that defines the U.S. diplomatic, military and economic position in a post-"post-Cold War" world. Those are the visions that can make a difference.

THE TWO CAVEATS

Having aired out the issue of "mission," let's look again at the challenge of implementation. I've quoted Powell to the effect that nothing is more important than clarity and consistency in mission. But, as we've seen in Chapter 3, that doesn't mean that a good leader must be inflexible—especially on the battlefield, where change and the unexpected are the only constants. So leaders honor their mission, but they are thoughtful and flexible in how they achieve it.

For example, as Powell and the rest of the Bush administration began shaping their response to the September 2001 terrorist attacks, they realized that certain long-standing U.S. policies were likely to get in the way of achieving the mission. Certain countries that we had chosen not to do business with, for example, now needed to be courted to join a worldwide coalition against terrorism. And certain kinds of operatives— specifically, those who in the past had been involved in the violation of human rights—would also have to be enlisted in the cause. The Bush administration willingly embraced these tactical changes, and also made a point of trying to bring the American public along.

This is mostly about *flexibility*, as opposed to compromising basic principles. Leaders shouldn't get so committed to one plan of execution that they can't see a new and better way to get to the same goal. Nor should they be so consumed by one goal that they lose the capacity to notice new opportunities along the way to the core objective. Their overarching vision, in other words, shouldn't negate their peripheral vision. There are times when these "side issues" push themselves to the front of the line, and emerge as missions worthy of being pursued in their own right.

So be flexible. Commitment is noble; rigidity is not. Dump tactics that aren't working. Pounce upon new opportunities that present themselves along the way to your stated goals. As Powell has told his people at State:

> *[Once] we have looked at all the rough edges*
> *and we have made a decision as to what we*
> *are going to do, then we are all going to*
> *move out in that decision and stick with it,*
> *with coherence and consistency over time,*
> *unless it has been proven that we should*
> *move in a different direction.*

Commitment and flexibility: It's the blend that counts. Be willing to capitalize on opportunities, but don't get distracted or spread too thin. Ask yourself, "Can this new opportunity be elevated to mission level, and earn that kind of commitment? If not, can we pursue it aggressively without getting distracted from our core mission, or without getting spread so thin that we can't pursue *anything* effectively?" For a corporation, there's nothing wrong with diversification, nothing wrong with initial probes of a market opportunity. But at the end of the day, leaders must feel confident about the mission, the resolve, the unit's commitment, and the resources to pursue total victory. That means leaders must be careful and selective in what they pursue. Scattering the enterprise's focus and energy weakens it. Organizations that are committed to everything are committed to nothing.

There's another caveat implicit in Powell's philosophy that I want to put on the table here. When it comes to implementation, *passionate commitment to a cause must be tempered by tactical prudence*. Great national causes are worth dying for, but the cause isn't served by unnecessary deaths. *"C'est magnifique,"* as the French Marshal Pierre Bosquet commented, watching the Light Brigade charge to its own destruction, *"mais ce n'est pas la guerre."* ("It's magnificent, but it's not war.") Don't let passion evolve into blind dogma or intractable zealousness that will lead to fatal errors in judgment. Going in for the kill is the right thing to do when it's *tactically* correct—not necessarily when passions are at their highest.

In both military and business battlefields, there are times to "zig and zag," rather than plunging straight ahead. There are times when you should cut your losses and beat a retreat, if that's what it takes to get some necessary reinforcements. There may be times when you need to provisionally accept unpleasant restrictions and strange bedfellows, if that's what it takes to advance toward the overall objective. As long as you don't ever lose sight of your final objectives, as long as you are (and you are understood to be) relentless in their pursuit, such actions are wise.

Powell has been criticized for compromising. That's a simple misreading of what Powell is actually about. In fact, his

career success has been built on a thoroughgoing commitment to mission, tempered by a clear-eyed prudence. In his
biography of Powell, Howard Means quoted Powell's colleague, retired Colonel Raymond "Red" Barrett, who was
asked how he responded to the assertion that Powell was a
political animal, without any particular belief system.
Nonsense, Barrett replied: Not only did Powell have strong
beliefs, but Barrett was glad that Powell was in a position of
power "because he won't compromise." Then Barrett cor-
rected himself: "That's a misstatement: he won't compromise
on the important things."

Set the goal, push, and "compromise" when backing off
advances the mission. Early in his career, in response to an
Army initiative to curb excessive drinking, Powell decided to
prohibit drinking altogether within his brigade, and shut
down the local watering hole. In the end, he was told to
reopen the club. Although he felt that reopening the club was
wrong for an institution that was trying to curb drinking, he
did so because he understood the club's importance for
morale, and because he didn't feel the fight was that critical.
"I did not want to make it my last fight. You cannot slay the
dragon every day. Some days the dragon wins."

Leaders need to tactically bob and weave in response to
emerging events, and even take a step sideways or back occasionally—provided, of course, that they stay in relentless pursuit of their final mission.

SIMPLICITY: A KEY POWELL
SUCCESS FACTOR

There is one more imperative associated with Powell's lessons
on mission and leadership: *Simplify*. On a daily basis, cut
through the morass of argument, debate, and doubt that

sometimes accompanies mission-related debates. Offer solutions that are clear and understandable. Simplification boosts clarity, focus, and the capacity to execute.

Whether it's in the realm of mission values, policies, performance standards, or appropriate conduct, *keep it simple.* The world is chaotic, complicated, and murky. In that context, your personal laser beam (of principles, of commitment, of purpose) will help get your team home safely. When Powell tells his direct report that a top priority is making the State Department Internet-ready and Internet-friendly for everyone, he's simplifying. When Powell also tells them "I expect you to convey upward to me the problems in your organizations, the aspirations in your organization, the needs of your organization. I expect you to protect your people, to defend your people, and fight for your people all the way up to me"—he's simplifying. The simplicity of these priorities makes it easier to develop and follow up with clear, logical, (even inspiring) goals and standards. When a leader makes the complex simple, people can more readily mobilize to achieve the extraordinary.

"If you can't explain it to your mother," suggests Air Force Colonel Hoot Gibson, "maybe you don't really understand it." A friend of Powell has observed that Powell's presentations are "all simple. There's no great 'Kissingerian' framework, but it's entirely solid and without fluff. It's entirely him."

Hence, here's a standard against which you can (and should) hold your organization: *How clear is your language?* If you, as a leader, can't make your case in simple and powerful terms, you haven't done your homework. Or, worse, you're tacitly admitting that you may be best served by a little obfuscation.

And one last principle that grows out of and reinforces simplicity: *Be consistent.* Consistency builds a leader's credibility and effectiveness. Powell is stunningly consistent. I benefited personally from that consistency: The philosophy he articulated in a speech ten years ago is essentially the same philosophy he advocates today. Just as important (perhaps even more important), Powell's actions are consistent with his words. Whatever he has done, be it on the field of battle or in the world of international diplomacy, seems to be readily consistent with one of the leadership lessons he has espoused for years. Yes, as he himself has pointed out, he's willing to shift tactical directions in line with new compelling data, but I've found that even a change in Powell's tactical direction is always consistent with his core values and philosophies. And once he shifts direction, he does so candidly and he stays the course. The bottom line is that there is a certain sustained bedrock foundation to Powell's leadership. It's easier for the troops to follow you (literally and figuratively) if you get up and say the same things every day.

When you look at the Powell record, you find remarkably little subterfuge, double dealing, cloudiness, smoke blowing, spinning, or expediency. Like most effective leaders, Powell discovered early on that there is tremendous strength to be derived from clarity, simplicity, and consistency.

SUMMARY

The message of this chapter is straightforward: State the mission in a way that is simple, clear, and understandable, and that is linked to the resources and tactics that are available to your organization. Then go after your goal with everything you've got. Good leaders cut through the bureaucracy, the politics, the mush, and the mud. They state the mission, sign up their recruits, and *implement*.

Strategy and management are sometimes made overly complicated. Overcomplication can lead to failure. How else can we explain an organization that is populated by highly intelligent managers, advised by consultants and academics, armed with elaborate planning documents and organizational policies based on complex theory, analysis, scenarios, and projections—that fails?

I haven't done a formal survey, but I think it's safe to assert that there have been no *Fortune* 500 companies since, say, 1980 that didn't have the benefit of an enormous planning effort—and, as we've already seen, a sizable percentage of those once-proud companies are no longer with us. True, some have merged and morphed into new entities. But that's a whole other realm of confusion and, quite often, embarrassments. Depending on the definitions you use and the lines you draw, somewhere between three-fifths and four-fifths of corporate mega-mergers—outlined with plans of impeccable depth, and fueled by financial wizardry—actually diminish shareholder value.

I don't necessarily advocate shutting down the planning departments. But I do think that good leaders take care to make sure that their organizations stay focused on the fundamental questions confronting them: Who are we? What do we stand for? What makes us great? What makes us unique? What do we hold dear? What binds us together? What are we trying to become? Where do we want to go? Where *will* we go? Where's our line in the sand?

Effective leaders take the abstract and complex and render it into something that is graspable and straightforward. They articulate vivid, overarching goals and values, which they use to drive daily behaviors and make choices among competing alternatives. Their visions and priorities are lean and compelling, not cluttered and complicated. Their decisions are crisp and clear, not tentative and ambiguous. Even while they're tactically flexible, they convey an unwavering firmness and consistency in their actions, aligned with the picture of the future that they are so carefully painting.

The result? Strength of purpose, credibility of leadership, integrity in organization, and a consistent record of accomplishment.

POWELL PRINCIPLES

1. **Execution is the key.** Do not articulate a vision or a mission unless you are prepared to implement it with overwhelming strength. Stay cool under fire, think big, act fast, and go for the big win.

2. **Pick your battles.** Elevate to mission status only those causes that are vital to the organization's success. You can't slay the dragon every day. Make sure that you choose your battles carefully.

3. **Remain flexible.** Pick your battles, but don't turn up your nose at opportunity. And even after you've settled on a winning strategy and tactics, be prepared to throw the game plan out the window in response to fast-moving circumstances.

4. **Remember Powell's Three Cs—clarity, consistency, and commitment.** When you are clear, consistent, and committed, you lend enormous strength to your organization. You also build your own credibility and authority, which is another plus for the organization. Never stop articulating and living the message, up and down the hierarchy.

5. **Keep it simple.** Simple messages are the best messages. Master the most complicated version of the story, but put a far simpler version of that story out in the field for general consumption. When someone needs more, they'll let you know.

PEOPLE
OVER PLANS

"Plans don't accomplish work.
Goal charts on walls don't
accomplish work.... It is people
who get things done."

COLIN POWELL likes to quote Hyman Rickover, the fabled Navy admiral who made a career of going up against established interests:

"Organization doesn't really accomplish anything. Plans don't accomplish anything either. Theories of management don't much matter. Endeavors succeed or fail because of the people involved."

Powell has his own homegrown version of the same basic idea. As he puts it: "Plans don't accomplish work. Goal charts on walls don't accomplish work. Even talking papers don't accomplish work. It is people who get things done."

People are the flip side of the "mission" coin. People breathe life into missions—and, for that matter, into plans, talking papers, and goal charts on walls. At the end of the day, people are why the mission (and eventually the enterprise itself) rises or falls. If people are not inspired and capable, if discipline and morale are low, if people don't have a sense of purpose, then the most elegant strategic plans and the most rational organizational designs won't make much difference.

Vision, even compellingly articulated vision, only gets you so far. Great people are the key. It is the led who ultimately validate the leaders. As Powell has said:

> *I don't know that leadership in the twenty-first century will be essentially different from the leadership shown by Thomas Jefferson, George Washington, and their colleagues 200 years ago. Leadership will always require people who have a vision of where they wish to take 'the led.' Leadership will always require people who are able to organize the effort of (others) to accomplish the objectives that flow from the vision.*

PEOPLE MAKE VICTORIES POSSIBLE

Some Powell observers have expressed surprise at his blunt skepticism about plans and organizations. I've never seen any evidence that Powell thinks we can do without these tools and structures, but he's relentlessly critical of lengthy, minutiae-riddled plans. "No battle plan," he says pointedly, "survives contact with the enemy." And he is quick to fault organizations that are more absorbed with internal issues (for example, with rank, titles, perks, and entitlements) than with mission and performance.

Consider the 1990 war against Iraq, which was the context in which Powell's star really started to rise. Most observers agree that the U.S.-led international victory in the Persian

Gulf had very little to do with either strategic planning or organizational design, *per se*. Yes, at the outset of the conflict, the Western leaders and their allies generated a credible plan. The plan included basic contingency scenarios for defense and attack, as well as a blueprint for logistics and other necessary preparations for battle readiness. Those steps were essential to spurring movement in the right directions. But by all subsequent accounts, they did little to secure the actual victory.

In fact, many of the original planning assumptions—about Iraqi defense positions, the legendary prowess of Saddam Hussein's crack Republican Guard, and projections of American casualties—turned out to be flat wrong. (And one could go back even further, to the U.S. military's late 1980s planning scenarios for the region, which failed to anticipate either the Iraqi invasion of Kuwait or the possibility of a viable U.S.-Saudi Arabian-Syrian coalition.) Instead of things following the script, there were surprises (mostly good ones) all up and down the line. When it was all over, General Norman Schwarzkopf, the field commander in the Gulf, commented that "we certainly did not expect the war to go this way."

So where did victory in the Gulf War come from? Once again, from *mission* and *people*, with particular emphasis on the latter. Victory came from "people intangibles"—from things like a fervently held purpose; hustle and responsiveness; large doses of no-sacred-cows imagination and responsibility in the field; unprecedented levels of all-hands, cross-unit collaboration; and a high percentage of team-player leaders. One Army officer summarized the Gulf War this way: "Technology didn't win this war. People did. Highly trained, highly motivated, and well-led people."

When prescribing for a military audience, Powell makes the point that "they [soldiers, pilots, sailors, Marines] all must believe that they are part of a team, a joint team, that fights together to win." And when he talks to leaders of business organizations, he advocates for a "people-centered" organization: "The most important assets you have in all of this are the people, and if you don't put people at the center of your process, you'll fail. Not profit motives, not size of the organization's headquarters, but people."

What differentiates successful companies from unsuccessful companies is rarely the brilliant, secret, take-the-market-by-storm grand plan. Indeed, the leaders of today's great companies are inclined to freely share their plans and business models in books and magazines. Even if they weren't, today's fast-moving economy dictates that most organizations' plans are on their way to obsolescence almost from the moment that they are publicly revealed.

The key to success, therefore, lies in exceptional, innovative, fast execution. Execution lies, in turn, in the capacity of people to quickly capitalize on fleeting opportunities in the marketplace; develop imaginative ideas and creative responses; generate fast, constantly changing action plans; mobilize teams and resources; get the job done swiftly and effectively—and then continue that process with relentless commitment.

That's what this "people" thing is all about, because it's people that make all that happen. What effective leaders do is create an environment in which great people can flourish in optimal pursuit of the enterprise's mission. In describing the famed symphony conductor Leonard Bernstein, one observer noted that "what Bernstein achieved—and what great leaders achieve—is a seeming paradox. He convinced his players they were free to innovate and express themselves, while convincing them to accept his vision for the music and to follow his direction." That description nicely captures the spirit of the leader role that Powell endorses.

POWELL'S DUAL PREMISES

When trying to get the most out of the people under his command, Powell adheres to two interrelated premises:

1. **People are competent.** As Powell once observed: "Officers have been trying for hundreds of years to outsmart soldiers, and have still not learned that it cannot be done. We can always count on the native ingenuity of the American GI to save us from ourselves and to win wars." Throughout his career, Powell has resisted the calls for quick-fix interventions designed by outsiders that are done, in his words, to people rather than for people. He sees outsider's contol as a last resort rather than as a first.

   To put it more positively, Powell regularly expresses his confidence in his people's ability to solve their own problems, and to use their experience and expertise to help the organization attain its goals. I've already mentioned the incident in which he brought in desk officers in Mexico to brief President George W. Bush directly. Surely Powell was trying to make a statement with this noteworthy departure from tradition. But just as surely, he was convinced that President Bush would get a better briefing from the desk officers. "That kind of reaching down," commented a State Department careerist, "really made people realize that Secretary Powell thinks he has an organization with talent at all levels."

> *Our ability to successfully perform our mission depends, first and foremost, on the quality of our people.... We're all part of one quality family, working together as a family. No component more important than any other component.*

That brings us to our second premise:

2. **Every task is important.** In one of his early speeches to State Department staff, Powell proclaimed:

> *I also believe, to the depth of my heart,*
> *that there is no job in the State Department*
> *that is unimportant. I believe that everybody*
> *has a vital role to play, and it is my job to*
> *communicate and convey down through*
> *every layer to the last person in the*
> *organization, the valuable role that they are*
> *performing and how what they do contributes*
> *to the mission. We have to be linked.*

Many managers pay lip service to this philosophy, but don't live it. Powell lives it. Marshall Adair, president of the American Foreign Service Association, believes that it was Powell's military background that taught him that every task counts, and that high morale is critical to getting the best out of people. That's why Powell goes out of his way to hammer home his message at every opportunity.

Once, when his plane stopped in Israel in the middle of a round of delicate talks with leaders in the volatile Mideast, Powell asked for twenty minutes to speak to the assembled staff of the U.S. Embassy at the Tel Aviv airport. Among other things, Powell praised the diplomats for carrying out their duties in dangerous places, and for serving on the front lines of U.S. foreign policy. Then he mingled with the "troops" until his departure time. One thrilled staffer, obviously amazed at the event, said that in her twenty-year career at State, she had never before shaken the hand of the secretary. "I never saw anything like this," confirmed one of her colleagues.

To some extent, Powell aims for the self-fulfilling prophecy. If you believe that your people are high performers and you convey that belief to them, they are likely to *be* high performers. "Powell aims to rally the troops at the State Department," says Brian Friel of *Government Executive*, "and turn the Foreign Service into a well-oiled diplomatic machine on the front lines of American international relations." Armed with this well-oiled machine, Powell believes he can turn the State Department into a far more potent force, devising better foreign policies and implementing those policies far more effectively.

Some might say that this is just common sense. But the fact is the State Department before Powell didn't tend to use people in a way that captured this "common sense." The "Old State" honored the titled dignitary and effectively ignored the input of individuals who had spent most of their working lives studying and working on the problem at hand. If they were bold enough to push themselves forward with an informed insight, they were very likely to get marginalized, or even derailed. Powell set out to turn this entrenched culture on its head, making sure that the best insights would be harvested and used by the system.

PEOPLE AND EXECUTION: TWO SIDES OF A COIN

To reiterate this major point: Powell doesn't put his emphasis on people for soft and fuzzy reasons, or to protect his "nice guy" reputation. By most accounts, he is a compassionate person who demonstrates his personal concern for, and interest in, the people who work for him. He makes them feel valued, inquires about their needs and personal lives, and sends letters to their families in times of personal crisis or in the wake of a hard-won individual victory.

But as we've seen in earlier chapters, Powell believes that a leader's top priority is to define a course of action and carry it through. That can happen only through people; therefore, taking good care of his people is the only way he can help his organization *implement*. And it's no slight to Powell to suggest that, like any smart leader, he may be taking good care of his people in part to enhance his own career and reputation.

If the people at State achieve miracles during Powell's stay there, then Powell will get credit for being a miracle worker. So "taking care of your people" has little to do with unconditional love, and may even be motivated by a dose of self-interest, but it has everything to do with harnessing the power of people to achieve a meaningful goal.

The skeptical reader might be inclined to challenge Powell on the second point of his people-management philosophy. If all tasks are important, the skeptic might say, then what happens when it comes time to cut the payroll? And what happens to the elevator operator when some smart guy comes up with an automated elevator?

Powell has certainly dealt with this circumstance, and on a large scale. Both as commander of FORSCOM (U.S. Forces Command) in the late 1980s and as chairman of the Joint Chiefs of Staff in the early 1990s, Powell was at the forefront in presenting the case for shrinking the military and creating a radically different fighting machine—leaner, faster, and more versatile. The fast-changing geopolitical environment called for nothing less. In one presentation on this theme, Powell imagined a world in which the old Soviet colossus had been dismembered, and free-market economics were playing a far more important role in geopolitics:

> *We've got to spend wisely and well. We have*
> *to put a hard question to ourselves before*

others put it to us: Do we need this item?
And when the answer is no, we have to say
no. Our challenge is to accept that we have
to retrench, yet continue to maintain the best
damned Army in the world.

Item cuts, Powell has argued, include job cuts. Good leaders begin with the premise that everyone's job is important, *but*, if new data demonstrate that a particular job becomes unimportant, they don't hold on to it (as is done in growing, bloated bureaucracies); they cut it. Sooner or later, the elevator operator's job will be obsolete. (Sooner or later, *all* of our jobs will be obsolete, which is why we have to keep changing our personal skill sets.) But the key is to *separate the job from the individual.* If a particular task or job has become outmoded or redundant, get rid of it. After six months on the job at State, for example, Powell had already cut a number of special envoy positions from the State Department payroll and returned the duties of those positions to the bureaus responsible for those areas.

Separate the job from the individual. Assess the job, and decide whether it needs to stay. Then assess the individual who has held that job. Can he or she be challenged in a new way? Can he or she step sideways into a job that will be ongoing? Can he or she be promoted? If the answer to these questions is consistently no, then it is time to cut the cord:

If you don't fire people who are not doing the
job—after you have counseled them, after
you have brought them along—then you're
hurting the whole organization.

People sometimes assume that the military provides lifetime employment (or at least employment long enough to secure a pension and lifetime benefits). In fact, the opposite is true, especially as one begins to climb into the military's upper reaches. Someone who fails to get promoted is almost certain to be moved out. In one interview, Powell revealed how the Army's up-or-out rules were explained to him, in very explicit terms:

> *The day I was promoted to three stars,*
> *a letter arrived from the chief of staff of*
> *the Army, the chairman of my corporation.*
> *The letter said, 'Dear Colin: Congratulations.*
> *You're three stars, and you are going to be*
> *a corps commander in Germany. You will*
> *hold that position for two years. If in two*
> *years, you have not heard from me offering*
> *you a second position or promoting you*
> *to four stars, I expect you to have your*
> *resignation on my desk.'*

As Powell subsequently elaborated: "He expected me to retire if he couldn't use me anymore. One job. If I did well and got another job, fine. If not, I had to keep things moving and make way for youngsters." In other words, as long as Powell was growing and developing, and as long as he was contributing more to the organization than a fresh young talent was likely to contribute, he would be valued and nurtured by that organization. These are worthy criteria for any leader to apply to the people on his or her team.

So people are assumed to be competent—until proven otherwise. (And a regular assessment is indispensable.) Tasks are assumed to be important—until proven otherwise. Good leaders see no contradiction between holding these beliefs and adhering to the principles espoused in this chapter. In fact, it's the capacity to subscribe to both of these apparently contradictory views at once that defines effective people management.

THE REAL STRATEGIC PRIORITY

In his military days, Powell would tell the new officers who were assigned to his command that he had two top priorities: "war-fighting and stewardship." In other words, he would do whatever it took to "accomplish the mission and look after the troops." By bundling these two concepts—by never invoking the one without the other—he was telling his new "middle managers" that policy and people were inseparable parts of the same strategy. In today's knowledge-based, "nanosecond" environment, leaders can no longer separate discussions about competitive advantage from discussions about people.

> *You give me the right people, and I don't much care what organization you give me. Good things will happen. Give me the wrong people, and it doesn't matter what you do with the organization. Bad things will happen.*

"Only by attracting the best people," observed Admiral Rickover, "will you accomplish great deeds." Powell agrees. So does Dell Computer CEO Michael Dell, who once told me that one of his top strategic priorities was attracting and retaining the best people. I took note of his use of the word *strategic*, as opposed to *human resource* or *personnel*. As many savvy executives have discovered, people aren't just a piece of the puzzle, they *are* the puzzle. Or, more accurately, they're the solution to the puzzle.

Jack Welch, recently retired from General Electric, says that GE's core competence is not lightbulbs, but *people*. Informal surveys suggest that highly effective executives like Michael Dell and Jack Welch spend between 50 and 75 percent of their time on "people" issues: recruiting, interviewing, assessing performance, developing reward systems, improving work environments, getting involved in training and development, and so on.

Many traditionalists who currently hold management positions will find it difficult to understand Dell's and Welch's calendars (over half their time on people issues?!), just as they will find it difficult to understand the concept that the stewardship of people should be a *strategic* priority. Too often, what happens in organizations is what typically occurred in the *pre*-Powell State Department. "It takes a new team a few months to get acquainted with the department, to get personnel appointed," says Bruce Laingen, president of the American Academy of Diplomacy. "Then they become preoccupied with day-to-day foreign policy challenges." The heat of battle intensifies, and the people issues (which seem easy to put off for another day) drop down the priority list.

The same scenario unfolds in the private sector. We've all heard the expression "Our most important assets are our people" so often that it's become trite. But how many corporate leaders really 'walk the talk'? Too often, people are assumed to be empty chess pieces to be moved around at will, which may explain why so many top managers immerse their calendar time in dealmaking, restructuring and the latest management fad. How many immerse themselves in the goal of creating an environment where people flourish? How many act as if their people are their primary source of competitive advantage?

Powell does, which is why he told an enthusiastic State Department audience in his first week on the job: "I'm not just coming in to serve the foreign policy needs of the American people, I'm coming in as the leader and the manager of this department." Policy is critically important. But Powell believes that the quality of policy and the capacity to execute policy with excellence are fueled by high morale, esprit de corps, personal initiative and skill levels at all levels of the organization.

THE SECRETS OF PARTNERSHIP AND "SERVANT LEADERSHIP"

In addition to pursuing the two aspects of the philosophy outlined above—people are competent, and their tasks are important—Powell employs two additional techniques for making his people a source of competitive advantage. First, he treats people as partners. Second, he embodies the concept of "servant leadership." Let's briefly look at each of these techniques:

1. **People as partners.** When Powell describes his style as "collegial," he's going well beyond the surface attributes of accessibility, civility, and open-door listening. He's identifying a particular way in which he treats people. He treats them not as subordinates who are expected to follow him blindly, but as partners who will bring their experience and expertise to the table, and who will work *with* him to achieve exceptional goals. Powell's new relationships with—*and higher expectations of*—desk officers and other mid-level staff professionals around the world are a case in point.

   In the old model at State, a small elite conferred, set policy, and issued directives to their underlings. In the model Powell put in place shortly after becoming secretary of state, he meets with his top forty managers every morning from 8:30 to 9:00. At that meeting, which is conducted at a brisk pace, people discuss issues, policies, and concerns—and then agree how to delegate to ensure the most effective possible implementation, and how they will follow up on that implementation. Every day, the pattern is the same: involvement, collaboration, formulation, delegation, and follow-up.

The new partnership model has reinvigorated many State careerists, who are now motivated to contribute to solving the organization's many problems. "The difference now," as one insider notes, "is that there is finally a critical mass of people in this building who are prepared to stop complaining and do something about it."

2. **Servant leadership.** As noted in a previous chapter, Powell faithfully observes a basic tenet of effective military leadership: Leaders are nothing without followers. Wal-Mart founder Sam Walton used to say, "The best leader is the servant leader." And there's a causal relationship here that should not be overlooked: If you work hard for your people, you make them stronger and more competent, which in turn makes *you* more effective.

Words are cheap, and lots of leaders call themselves "servants." But the best of them believe and live by this philosophy. "These people are fantastic people," says Herb Kelleher of his former colleagues at Southwest Air, which has more or less sailed above the problems facing the airline industry in recent years. "You want to work hard for them."

Powell feels the same about *his* employees. That's why he will take twenty minutes to thank State employees at an Israeli airport. That's why he has pushed so hard to get fully secure, state-of-the-art Internet capability for every employee. That's why he has focused on getting funds for more employee training and management development. And that's why he's taking action on long-standing State Department employee concerns, such as quality child care and programs aimed at helping Foreign Service officers' spouses find work overseas.

When Powell was commander of V Corps in Germany, he told his troops that he would fight tenaciously for everything they needed to perform the mission. "If we don't have it in Frankfurt," he told them, "I'll go to USAREUR [U.S. Army Europe]. If they don't have it, I'll go to Washington. But I will back you all the way." This is the essence of servant leadership.

I am going to fight for you. I am going to do
everything I can to make your job easier.

SUMMARY

Through his words—and also through his deeds—Powell makes a strong case that "the only way to accomplish your mission is through those troops entrusted to your care."

The effective leader believes that his or her people are competent, and that their tasks are important to the organization—until proven otherwise. The effective leader puts people in positions where they can excel and grow—and, of course, tracks and encourages their progress. And finally, the effective leader treats people as partners and finds ways to act as a "servant leader."

When all of these conditions are met, everyone grows, the organization prospers, and the leader's authority and credibility are reinforced. But it all begins and ends with *people*. "At the end of the day," Powell reminds us, " it's some soldier who will go up a hill and correct your mistakes and take that hill."

POWELL PRINCIPLES

1. **Count on people more than plans or structures.** Without great people who are empowered by supportive cultures, the best-laid plans are likely to be of little use.

2. **Assume that people are competent, and that every job counts, until proven otherwise.** There is no such thing as an unimportant job. Every role is vital, particularly in a world in which vigilance is the new imperative. If the data show otherwise, make changes. Where possible, retool and retrain before you fire.

3. **Spend at least 50 percent of your time on people.** Planning is clean and people management is messy, so leaders are tempted to hang out in the clean task neighborhoods. Don't succumb. People provide your competitive advantage, so spend significant parts of your workday insuring that the organization is an environment in which people can grow and flourish. Elevate tasks like recruiting, assessing performance, improving work environments, and developing competencies to the status of strategic priorities.

4. **View people as partners, regardless of their place in the hierarchy.** Like most effective leaders, Powell sees every person as a partner who brings experience and expertise to help him achieve exceptional goals.

5. **Become a servant leader. Work "for" your people.** Help people to accomplish the goals that emanate from the vision. Give them the tools they need, and turn them loose.

CHAPTER 9

VIGILANCE
IN DETAIL

*"If you are going to achieve excellence
in big things, you develop the habit
in little matters. Excellence is not
an exception, it is a prevailing attitude."*

TO UNDERSTAND POWELL'S emphasis on mastering details, it's necessary to begin with what I'll call, maybe indelicately, the "Holy Sh** Factor."

When Powell headed the Joint Chiefs of Staff under President George Bush Senior, he frequently played the part of the no-nonsense military realist. Sometimes he was called upon to do so when, in the face of a particularly knotty international problem, a gung-ho senior advisor or politician would propose a "let's-kick-them-in-the-butt" military solution. All heads would swing to Powell, of course, who would be asked to look into the proposal and brief the president and his inner circle on how the job might be carried out.

Powell would go off and do his homework. When it came time to revisit the subject, he would arrive at the meeting absolutely loaded to the gills with details, including contingency plans, costs, logistics, manpower needs, time frames, casualty assessments, and so on. And in a matter-of-fact tone, Powell would painstakingly review exactly what would be required to carry out this particular "let's-kick-them-in-the-butt" solution.

As Powell unveiled the details, some of his listeners would begin to experience the "Holy Sh**!" reaction. It became perfectly clear that what might have looked like an easy intervention (a "surgical strike," to invoke a phrase that Powell detests) would in fact be a large, complicated, and dangerous undertaking. And as the *Chicago Tribune* once noted dryly, after such a Powell presentation, subsequent interest in a purely military option was often greatly reduced.

Powell's attention to detail continues today as he puts his stamp on the sprawling empire that is the State Department. In a feature article in the late November, 2001 *New York Times* magazine, Bill Keller writes: "Those who have worked with him say that Powell is usually the best-prepared person in any meeting and has anticipated the arguments several steps out."

Preparation and discipline are essential for leadership, according to Powell, which is why he asserts, very simply: "Never neglect details." His perspective extends even to "big-picture" vision and mission. The Powell doctrine, discussed in chapter 7, describes how leaders formulate and execute a successful mission. Ambassador Tom Graham, who has worked with Powell, observes that "the Powell doctrine requires a certain amount of time and deliberation before taking action."

Time and deliberation is emphatically not a stalling tactic. It's not a "let's-have-another-study" hesitancy, or an expression of "let's-buy-some-more-time" timidity. On the contrary: Throughout his career, Powell has been the one who has looked his people in the eye and said, "No more studies!"

And it's safe to venture that Powell's star would have never risen as dramatically as it has had he acted with tentativeness or hypercaution.

Instead, as we've seen in an earlier chapter, the Powell doctrine is about carving out a clear mission, then pursuing its objectives decisively. But it's also about mastering the details before you launch a campaign.

DETAILS CAN HELP WITH THE BIG PICTURE

There are lots of reasons to do so. First of all, as George Bush Sr.'s cabinet discovered more than once, with Powell's help, the details will absolutely change the way you think about your options. And once you've settled on a particular option, mastery of the details leads to better execution and increased unit cohesion. And, not least important, the leader who has clearly mastered the details inspires confidence. "When he briefed me," the senior President Bush once commented, "I found there was something about the quiet, efficient way he laid everything out and answered questions that reduced my fears and gave me great confidence."

I remember having that same reaction on September 13, 2001, two days after the terrorist attack, as I watched Powell at a nationally televised news conference. Yes, I was reassured by his clear mission: "We will rip up that (al-Qaeda) network and have a global assault on terrorism." On its own, however, that statement would be in danger of being simply an empty gung-ho declaration. I was doubly reassured that Powell coupled his mission statement with a calm assertion that he and the Bush team would be focusing relentless attention on quickly gathering "details, information, and evidence" in order to identify the right targets, the right allies, the right courses of action, and so on.

Attending to details has additional benefits. As chairman of the Joint Chiefs of Staff, Powell once observed that watching the small things can help accomplish two goals: It tells a commander the true state of readiness (rather than how things look on the surface), and "a general's attention to detail lets the soldier far down the chain know that his link is as vital as the one that precedes or follows."

This was a lesson that he had learned decades earlier. In January of 1964, Powell was filling up the time between assignments by taking an advanced Pathfinder training course. (Pathfinders are elite parachutists who jump in ahead of their airborne units to mark landing and drop zones.) During the very last flight, on a cold January evening, Powell, as senior officer, instructed his classmates to check their static lines, which are the lines that automatically open the parachute as the paratrooper jumps from the plane.

Minutes later, he ordered them to check their lines, and also the lines of their jumping partners, again. And a few more minutes later, shortly before the scheduled jump, he checked all of the lines himself. When he did so, he found one sergeant's line loose. Neither the sergeant, his jumping partner, nor the jumpmaster had noticed this crucial error. In that case, Powell's attention to detail averted only a potential individual tragedy, but it's easy to imagine how overlooking a tiny detail could jeopardize an entire mission. It's also easy to imagine the lesson that the Pathfinders took away from their encounter with Powell.

Aren't we talking about the self-evident again? Unfortunately, no. Senior executives are tugged in a thousand directions at once. "Big-picture" issues tend to overwhelm the details. (And indeed, one would fault the executive who neglected the big picture in favor of minutiae.) But the difficult fact remains that the big picture is made up of many details.

And unfortunately, when leaders ignore this reality, the devil in the details often rears its ugly head and creates havoc in the form of thoughtless, superficial, untimely, or myopic decisions. In the private sector, this occurs more often than we care to admit: inadequate due diligence prior to a big acquisition or capital expenditure, poor appraisal of competitors' movements prior to a major product launch, superficial awareness of customer or employee attitudes, naive conclusions on what it'll take to integrate newly purchased technologies with old systems and cultures, and so on. If you're not the master of the details, you can't be the master of the big picture.

Powell has always seemed to resonate to this principle. During his White House fellowship, Powell got another lesson in the importance of details. Preferring to spend his time as an officer commanding in the field, he had initially resisted accepting the fellowship that was offered to him. After thinking through the opportunity, though, he decided that it might provide an incomparable education in the inner workings of government. He guessed right, later describing his experience in the Office of Management and Budget as observing the "engine room of the government." If you want to understand something intimately, go to where the people are dealing with the details.

> *I have an insatiable demand to be in charge of the information flow. If you don't know what information is flowing through your organization, you don't know what's going on in your organization.*

Sometimes details are neglected because they're not sexy enough. Let's face it: Standing up on the bridge and scanning the far horizons usually has more appeal than hanging out in the engine room. Management guru Peter Drucker was once asked to explain a particular flurry of mergers and acquisitions (many of which turned out to be bad deals). "I will tell you a secret," he said in response. "Dealmaking beats working. Dealmaking is exciting and fun, and working is grubby. Running anything is primarily an enormous amount of grubby detail work and very little excitement, so dealmaking is kind of romantic, sexy. That's why you have deals that make no sense."

Good leaders don't view details (or the engine room) as grubby. They view the mastery of detail as an integral part of leadership. Consider what makes the exceptional athletic coaches—people like Phil Jackson and Bill Parcells. A big piece of their success derives from their *deep, personal* immersion in details, and their expectation that everyone around them will get immersed as well.

It's about *habit* and *attitude*. Powell puts it this way:

> **If you are going to achieve excellence**
> **in big things, you develop the habit in little**
> **matters. Excellence is not an exception,**
> **it is a prevailing attitude.**

DETAIL MANAGEMENT IS NOT MICROMANAGEMENT

Let's look a little more closely at what mastering detail is *not*. We already know that it is not an excuse for the proverbial "analysis paralysis." Attending to details with speed, thoroughness, and urgency is not the same as engaging in incessant cover-thy-rear research and meetings.

Nor is attention to detail a rationale for micromanaging, overcontrolling, or second-guessing the efforts of others. When Powell gathers data and otherwise attends to detail, he doesn't necessarily do it himself. He's happy to use staff; and he liberally delegates. (Every good leader does.) In fact, Powell regularly tells his staff at State that the relationship he has with the president of the United States—gathering and integrating data and making recommendations accordingly— is the same relationship he wants his team to have with him. President Bush wants to get great details from Powell, and Powell wants the same from his staff.

Good leaders not only pay attention to details as a necessary part of their work, but also create a process whereby others do so, too. You want *everybody* worrying about those static lines if you're about to jump out of that plane. As Powell told State Department employees in one of his first meetings with them:

> *Those of you who are leaders, I expect you to convey upward to me the problems in your organizations, the aspirations in your organization, the needs of your organization.*

And there's another piece to this. When he was chairman of the Joint Chiefs of Staff, Powell reported directly to Dick Cheney, who was then secretary of defense. One day early in Powell's tenure, Cheney took Powell aside and told him that while Powell was doing a good job, Cheney didn't appreciate the fact that *all* of his information was being funneled through Powell. As secretary of defense, Cheney said, he needed to be receiving information from lots of different sources.

Reflecting on this request, Powell acknowledged that Cheney had a valid point. Cheney needed a rich tapestry of details in order to construct his own big picture. Some of those details had to come from other places, or Cheney's big picture would be no different from Powell's. Powell took steps to change the information flow accordingly.

We've already talked about striking the balance between detail and the big picture. Another thing that mastery of detail is *not* is an abdication of big-picture thinking— although it's sometimes seen that way. Peter Drucker tells of a 2000-year-old Roman legal pronouncement that stated, loftily, "The magistrate does not consider trifles."

Well, assuming that the magistrate preferred to focus on the big picture rather than trifles, Powell wouldn't disagree totally with that pronouncement. In fact, you need someone smart worrying about the big picture. The "vision thing" is important. After all, what's the point of the details if you're not planning to go anywhere exciting with them? Absent a compelling mission or vision, the best that details can do is help a leader serve as a tactician.

All true, but at the same time, Powell doesn't buy into the faddish concept of the regal "visionary" leader, the kind who stays perched on a lofty pedestal, aloof and removed, having "delegated" all the "trifles" of his or her so-called "grand vision." Good leaders know there's no solid, successful "big picture" without the details. Both are essential—not only when the mission and strategy are being sketched out, but also when they are being implemented. Effective leaders commit to both vision and detail orientation.

Let's cite one other "is not." Being attentive to details *is not* an excuse for obsessive-compulsive behavior. There are many individuals in management positions whose concerns revolve around minutiae and routine, and who insist that the people around them maintain a rigid, go-by-the-book routine. When these obsessive types are in positions of power, they can cause great harm, especially when they drown their own people with minutiae.

Yes, obsessive-compulsive behavior is a kind of attention to detail, but it's a distorted kind of attention. At best, this kind of leadership yields the classic "not seeing the forest for the trees" kind of myopia. At worst, it dampens morale, dulls the mind, and drives out imagination and innovation, even as it encourages conformity and complacency. And, unfortunately, obsessive-compulsive behavior in some leaders arises when they and their organizations are under stress—in other words, at precisely the juncture when great leadership is most needed.

As Powell warns:

> **When everyone's mind is dulled or distracted**
> **the leader must be doubly vigilant.**

Yes, details can dull and distract people if that's all they have on their plate. But if they also have the vision clearly in sight—a compelling vision that their own detail orientation will help achieve—the organization can move forward aggressively.

DETAILS DICTATE DIRECTION

As noted above, two of the key reasons for attending to details are to *determine the best course of action* and to *implement that course of action with decisiveness, speed, and efficiency*. Let's review each of these in greater depth.

During his January 18, 2001, Senate confirmation hearings, Powell made the following comment about the Bush administration's philosophy regarding foreign policy:

> **We must be involved according to**
> **our national interests and not in some**
> **haphazard way that seems more dictated**
> **by the crisis of the day than by serious,**
> **thoughtful foreign policy.**

While Powell didn't say so in so many words, it's *details*—in the form of timely and relevant data, information, and knowledge—that minimize the risk of haphazard, flaky, or just plain wrong policy decisions. Of course the details will not by themselves generate the best solution or course of action, but paying attention to the details *will* increase the likelihood of sound analyses and creative insights. Exploring and making sense of messy details, especially those that don't support one's preconceptions, makes good leaders call on their synthesizing skills, which presumably are one reason why they're there in the first place.

Historian Stephen Ambrose notes that during World War II, General Dwight Eisenhower "had an insatiable curiosity for details. In the war, he always asked about the weather report—not just what the forecast was, but how his people came up with the forecast. If he hadn't questioned the weather, his landing at Omaha Beach would have proven to be incorrect, and he would not have landed troops there. You never know when small details will become the determining factor."

The transcripts of the military commanders' meetings before and during the Gulf War revealed how carefully Powell and Norman Schwarzkopf—the most senior executives of the command—paid attention to a constant flow of details: satellite photos, artillery movements, diplomatic maneuvers, and so on.

Another important aspect of that military campaign was how effectively Powell and Schwarzkopf used their mastery of these details to accelerate urgency, continually shift people's attention to the right places, and generate contingency plans on a rolling basis, in real time. The core mission ("free Kuwait") remained constant, but the tactics for achieving that mission changed almost constantly as new details arrived and were rapidly assimilated.

The analogy between war and business is inexact, of course. But like Schwarzkopf and Powell, business leaders who continually scan and monitor the ever-changing environment around them—for example, the details of changes in technology, customer expectations, competitors' movements, demographic trends, and so on—are in fact positioning their organizations for health and growth. The ability to make sense of those fleeting details and respond quickly and innovatively is also critical, which leads us to the next major point.

DISCIPLINE IN DETAILS IS DISCIPLINE IN EXECUTION

The second major reason for attending to details revolves around execution. As we've discussed earlier, effective strategy means little without the means for effective execution. In the context of this chapter, it's *attention to detail* that yields great execution. And in a very real sense, attention to detail is a form of discipline for leaders.

For most of his life, Powell was a military man, so he is inclined to embrace a discipline that advances the mission. But for Powell, discipline is not about hierarchy and blind obedience. It's about preparation and consistency. Remember the story of the Pathfinders? "Check small things," he constantly tells the people around him. It's an invaluable discipline. It gets the right information to the leader, and it gets good decisions from the leader back out into the organization. It permits, and even compels, follow-up and assessment, and recalibration when necessary. Details feed the iterative loop that makes for a responsive organization. But the loop doesn't happen by accident. It happens through the discipline that is imposed by the leader and embraced by the led.

When leaders remove themselves from the details that impact budgets, operations, customers, employees, and the like, they lose touch. Gradually, they lose connection with the people and activities they are supposed to be leading. They begin to rely almost entirely on second- and third-hand reports. They become dependent on "gatekeepers" who strive to protect them, and on obsequious staff who strive to win favor with them. Though they don't know it, their decisions are increasingly made in a vacuum. Relationships suffer. Accuracy of data suffers. Execution suffers.

In contrast, attention to details keeps leaders fully engaged, fully in touch, and fully "in the know" with their teams and their progress towards the mission.

SUMMARY

For many people in leadership, a "call to detail" is not exactly the most rousing battle cry. It somehow doesn't fit with their concept of a leader. Aren't leaders supposed to be above daily routine and humdrum concerns? Aren't there more important things that the leader should be doing?

As we've seen, the answer is both yes and no. The most successful leaders understand that vision and details are inseparable when one's enterprise is operating in a volatile, hyper-competitive environment. For Powell, whose hobby is fixing old Volvo's, this conclusion is obvious. Anyone who makes daily decisions which impact the entire planet, but who also says that "my idea of a good time is to disconnect every wire, tube, hose, cable, and bolt of an engine," is clearly a person who appreciates the fine interplay between details and big picture!

POWELL PRINCIPLES

1. **Master the details before and during the launch of a major project or campaign.** Powell's mastery of details has often played a decisive role in the most crucial decisions of government: waging war and keeping the peace. Do not make key decisions without the relevant facts and details.

2. **Use your mastery of details for great decisions and great execution.** By mastering the details, you can avoid major missteps, capitalize on superb opportunities, spur a sense of urgency, and get people focused on the right direction.

3. **Stay in touch with the "little" things.** As Powell put it: "If you are going to achieve excellence in big things, you develop the habit in little matters." Ultimately, it may be attention to the small matters that later translates into a key victory. Don't lose touch—especially as you ascend the hierarchy.

4. **Avoid "analysis paralysis."** Attending to the fine points is not a license to micromanage, hide from a decision, or become obsessive-compulsive. Making sure that you and your team members have the information they need is not an excuse to postpone or put off key decisions, nor is it a rationale for maintaining the status quo.

5. **Remember that discipline in details is discipline in strategy.** Details dictate direction. Sound strategy requires sound execution. Even the best ideas are useless if they cannot be implemented; therefore, the details (grubby as they often are) may well dictate the best course of action.

CHAPTER 10

SITUATION DICTATES STRATEGY

"Fit no stereotypes. Don't chase
the latest management fads.
The situation dictates which approach
best accomplishes the team's mission."

THROUGHOUT HIS CAREER, Colin Powell has resisted chasing the latest trend or fad. Repeatedly, he argues against falling into rigid patterns of behavior.

He is arguing for a *situational* approach to leadership. In other words, he is making the case that effective leadership depends on a thorough immersion in the here and now—on a precise understanding of the situation at hand. Anything that clouds that vision or impedes effective action—be it an organizational rut, a stereotyped behavior, or the embrace of a succession of management fads—hurts the organization. The landscape changes, says Powell; therefore, the effective leader is ever vigilant, ready to shift strategy and tactics as the situation warrants.

AVOID "ONE-SIZE-FITS-ALL" SOLUTIONS

One size *never* fits all. The same is true for management fads, which abound today in part because of the proliferation of business advisors and consultants, and because of managers who seek quick fixes to problems. Flitting from fad to fad, even when those fads come dressed in sophisticated business jargon and embody some sensible principles, is very likely to damage the organization's ability to achieve its mission. Faddism generates confusion about priorities, reduces the leader's credibility, and drains organizational coffers.

A foolish consistency, said Ralph Waldo Emerson, is the hobgoblin of little minds. No policy is forever. If the context changes dramatically, it is unlikely that your organization's established patterns of behavior will continue to be effective. For example, there are circumstances in which quality is all-important, but changing circumstances may push speed to market higher up the priority list. Sometimes organic growth makes more sense than growth by acquisition, but in other economic environments, the opposite is true.

The same goes for individual styles. When a leader engages in what I call stereotypical behavior—in other words, constantly using a particular style or approach to lead people—that, too, can be damaging, for it very often generates rigidity in thought and action. One's favorite style or approach may not fit the unique demands of the situation. Sometimes giving an unapologetic directive is more appropriate than calling for participatory discussion—like in crisis, in the heat of battle, when participants are inexperienced, or when participatory discussion gets bogged down. But just to muddle things further, some situations are better served by discussion even in times of crisis and battle and such. It all depends, and good leaders scope out the situation accordingly.

This is why Powell has little patience with buzzwords and catch phrases, such as "empowerment" and "power down." These are the phrases of *formula*. But in most cases that involve humans in organizations, formulas don't apply. Some situations require the leader to hover closely; others require long loose leashes. Management techniques are not magic elixirs, but simply tools that wise leaders reach for at the right times, and then put back on the shelf.

Powell has repeatedly told his staff, his interviewers, and his audiences that he can't be pegged and won't be stereotyped. He is wary of anyone—colleague or consultant—who promotes a fad or a "one-best-way" approach. Let the situation dictate the needs, he believes, and let the leader figure out the best course of action to accomplish the mission.

> *Vogue phrases such as 'power down'*
> *and 'centralized versus decentralized*
> *management' were not part of my*
> *vocabulary. I would give [my*
> *direct reports] whatever help was*
> *needed to get the job done.*

Let's be very clear: Powell is not suggesting that leaders operate in an "anything goes" philosophical vacuum. Nor is he suggesting that leadership can be boiled down to a completely opportunistic, value-free "ends-justify-the-means" process. The opposite is true: The lessons in this book constitute a clear strategic, philosophical, value-based, and ethical blueprint by which Powell leads. The blueprint guides him; he lives it and endorses it. But the blueprint has enormous flexibility and creative opportunity built into it. If you get to the bridge and the bridge is out, you go look for another bridge—while still aiming for the same destination.

FLEXIBILITY IN ACTION:
A KEY POWELL TRAIT

Consider the following three scenarios. Do any of these sound like they could happen in your organization?

Scenario 1: Management rolls out a new business initiative. It doesn't much matter whether this particular initiative focuses on e-commerce, quality, customer service, diversity, or whatever. No matter what the focus of the initiative, across the organization, the troops groan. They know what is sure to follow, because they've seen it all before. The speeches will be made in the atrium, the hand-outs will be handed out, the training session will be held—and that will be it. Even before the helium has entirely escaped from the launch-related balloons, things are getting back to normal. Like the balloons, the initiative slowly deflates. The only real threat to the established order is that the leader is sure to read another tract by a management guru, or attend another seminar. Then the cycle will begin again: The next initiative sweeps through the office, and everyone dives for bureaucratic cover.

Scenario 2: Top management decides that the organization's leaders must back off from being so "hard" on things like performance, accountability, and results. Instead, they must learn to be better listeners, better facilitators, and better communicators. They must learn to be more sensitive to their people's feelings and needs. They must learn to suggest and persuade, rather than demand and command.

Scenario 3: This is simply Scenario 2 flipped on its head, which still manages to make the same point. Top management decides that the organization's leaders must get "back to basics," which translates into getting tougher on people, imposing higher standards, and demanding more consistent performance. They must challenge incompetence, jump on failures, and be relentless about criticizing when criticism is needed. They must learn to *push*, to lay down the law, and to demand excellence.

What do these three scenarios have in common, and why do they contradict the Powell leadership style? The answer is that they are all *packaged responses to problems*. To Powell, leadership is a *calling*. It demands duty to mission, values, and people. This, in turn, means using one's full powers of flexibility and imagination to achieve the organization's ends. The organization and its people deserve no less from their leader.

And practical considerations only reinforce these philosophical underpinnings. External conditions are always in flux (there are always new competitors, new opportunities). Internal conditions also continually change (there are always new processes, new employees). And "when the environment changes," says Powell, "you have to change with it and try to get ahead of it."

Powell is certainly willing to change the way *he* thinks. As discussed in previous chapters, when Powell determined that the post-Cold War environment required a vastly different type of military, he personally did a 180-degree turn. While some of his peers persisted in following the same old approaches to planning for and managing the military, and others sought to apply Band-Aids in the form of cost efficiencies, "total quality," and "re-engineering," Powell threw out the playbook. He shifted his own direction, and eventually his organization's direction, in pursuit of a new military.

Generals, it is said, often fight the last war. That's understandable, especially when the last war led to glorious victory. But generals whose mindset is mired in the last war are likely to be defeated. Each engagement is different. Each situation needs to be examined, and responded to, on its own merits. Retired Marine Corps General Anthony Zinni believes that the 1990–1991 Gulf War, a collision of large forces on a clear battlefield, is already an anachronism. In fact, he says, "The only reason Desert Storm worked was because we managed to go up against the only jerk on the planet who actually was stupid enough to confront us symmetrically."

NEW WARS, NEW RULES

The ongoing war against terrorism, in which Powell is playing a prominent part, only underscores this point. Who and where are the enemies, for example? They can be anywhere within 60 countries, including the U.S. Their organization, notes a senior American intelligence officer, is such a loose amalgam of extremist groups and individuals that even eliminating one group of antagonists (say, the Taliban in Afghanistan) or taking out one individual (say, Osama bin Laden) will not end the problem. Their locations are very hard to track because they operate in tiny, mobile underground cells, often completely divorced from other cells in the network. Their finances might be stashed in Western banks, including American. Their weapons can be purchased on open markets, from friend or foe.

Their approach to battle is more furtive than that of guerillas, and more lethal, since their fear of death is negligible and their targets are everyday civilians. Their weapons might include airplanes, letters, chemicals, or cyber-tools (terrorism expert Frank Ciluffo has already noted in his congressional testimony: "While bin Laden may have his finger on the trigger, his grandson might have his finger on the mouse"). Clearly, the old stereotypical responses to warfare won't work because the new theatre is so vastly different.

Just as clearly, circumstances as different as these demand entirely new visions and new battle plans. They demand a heuristic, reality-based approach. "We don't *do* mountains," Powell has said pointedly, suggesting that the United States won't repeat the mistakes of the Soviet Union in Afghanistan. In other words, we are unlikely to see a massive deployment of hardware and personnel to a land characterized by inhospitable terrain and tenacious, experienced warriors. Instead, we will respond *situationally*. We will think small, flexible, and opportunistic. We will focus as much on freezing funds as on dropping bombs. We will emphasize diplomacy and education as much as (or more than) the seizure of territory. As syndicated columnist Thomas Friedman noted, the battles "have to be fought in schools, mosques, churches, and synagogues, and can be [won] only with the help of imams, rabbis, and priests."

Part of the educational process will occur at home, and will involve new definitions of victory. In this war (and perhaps in future wars) we are unlikely to witness formal surrender ceremonies on the decks of aircraft carriers. We are unlikely to see ceremonial swords handed from losing general to winning general. In a *New York Times* interview in October 2001, Powell described what he would call a successful conclusion to the campaign against terrorism: "I see the success of this campaign being measured in the restoration of a degree of security in society, where people are not as frightened as they are now."

This must be a difficult definition for a career military man to offer. Instead of expelling an aggressor from a conquered territory, we can make the world safer only by degrees—by tracking down today's terrorists, and by changing the circumstances that would otherwise breed future terrorists. This means using not only military action, but also diplomacy, economic sanctions and aid, and a host of other tools.

Victory will come, Powell told the *Times*, "when there is less terrorism, far less, preferably zero terrorism with a global reach of the world." In other words, says Powell, we have to *think differently*. We have to acknowledge a changed situation and work within it. We need not abandon our deeply held principles (that would constitute a true victory for our foes), but we may well have to abandon the strategies and tactics that we've long depended upon.

WE'RE ALL PLAYING
UNDER NEW RULES

I believe corporate leaders face similar challenges and opportunities on their own terrain, whether they know it (or acknowledge it) or not. Consider Powell's commentary on the demise of the Soviet empire, into which I've taken the liberty of inserting some private-sector analogues:

"It used to be that we had a unifying theory of the world; a coherent idea of the world [*i.e., conventional wisdom*]. The U.S. had a containment strategy towards communism and we all knew the rules of the road [*everyone in the industry, including our competitors, played by accepted rules*]. But the new Russian leader, Gorbachev, didn't follow the script [*a competitor started playing a new game, with new rules*].... He left the country in disarray [*familiar value propositions and value chains have been disrupted*], but there is no going back to the former system of government [*the old familiar marketplace and traditions are dying; there's no going back*]."

It doesn't matter whether you're a general or a CEO, a colonel or a division manager: You need to constantly change your approach to fit evolving situations. You can't become wedded to the Maginot Line—the supposedly impermeable barrier that the French threw up after World War I to keep out the Germans, but around which the Germans simply drove their newly mobile army. (The Maginot Line's designers anticipated the cavalry charges and trench warfare that had dominated wars up to that point.) Similarly, you can't become wedded to a particular business model, program, technique, style, or tool. Stay creative, flexible, and disciplined in pursuit of your goals.

Among his other positive traits, Powell is an immensely *practical* leader. "Problem solving is the core of leadership," he asserts. Practical, action-oriented, problem-solving leaders don't become prisoners to means. They eclectically focus on ends. They think on their feet. They improvise. They rely on other people's brains and initiatives, as well as their own. They understand that part of good leadership is the ability to employ the most effective tool for the situation at hand.

SUMMARY

One of the keys to Powell's philosophy is his emphasis on *flexibility* and *imagination*. Since conditions are always shifting, the leader must always be ready to shift also when conditions warrant it. The new war on terrorism is only the latest example. It demands a new mindset, new methods of operation, and perhaps even new definitions of victory. None of this is possible without flexibility and imagination, and the willingness to embrace change.

Yet let me insert a final word of caution. Flexibility, imagination and change can sometimes be exhausting and scary. As humans, we seek to minimize uncertainty, risk, and injury. When we band together in organizations, we carry these priorities forward. But sometimes these priorities become so extreme that leaders become drawn to the tantalizing promise of the quick fix. As those in the private sector who have suffered through the chairman's latest pet program can attest, management is often drawn to fads that offer the elusive promise of quick change and painless victory.

There are no quick or easy fixes. (If there were, we would not need leaders.) When all is said and done, observes Powell, "There are no secrets to success. It is the result of preparation, hard work, and learning from failure."

POWELL PRINCIPLES

1. **Do not manage by fad.** There are no magic elixirs that will suit every situation. A leader's job is to assess every situation and adopt the direction and course of action that best fits the situation. Don't become rigidly wedded to any process, tool, method, or technique.

2. **Be ready to change on a dime.** No leader should plan on constantly shaking things up and shifting strategy. On the other hand, the best leaders run enterprises that are fleet and flexible. Be prepared to change direction as the situation warrants it.

3. **Don't fight "the last war."** In times of uncertainty, don't assume that "back to basics" or some other popular buzzword tactic is the right course of action. Many leaders fall into the trap of returning to the familiar when things get rough. Don't cling to stereotypical responses just because you're comfortable with them.

4. **"Ride" change, rather than managing it.** It is better to create a fast, agile, flexible enterprise that can ride the waves of change than to build a seawall. It is impossible to

"manage" the unforeseeable. Effective organizations are prepared to respond to a wide variety of contingencies, and are flexible enough to implement new directions as necessary.

CHAPTER 11

POWELL'S RULES
FOR PICKING PEOPLE

*"Look for intelligence and
judgment and, most critically,
a capacity to anticipate,
to see around corners."*

HOW WILL YOU accomplish great deeds? "Only by attracting the best people," says Colin Powell.

Effective business leaders know exactly what Powell is talking about. As mentioned in an earlier chapter, Michael Dell says that attracting and retaining top talent is a key strategic priority for Dell Computer. Bill Gates is equally explicit. For years, he has asserted that Microsoft must always hire the smartest, most capable people. Even if there's no specific job open for them at the moment, Gates has said, hire them anyway. With guidance from leaders, they'll define their own job, and good things will happen.

The best people will develop the best ideas and the most effective follow-ups. They will develop the right technology and the optimal application for it. They will figure out how to use available resources to connect with one another to develop the most exciting products, the most extraordinary cost reductions, the most dazzling customer services, the most lucrative niches, and the most promising investment opportunities. They'll help you define and attain your mission in ways you couldn't have dreamed of on your own.

So (says Powell) surround yourself with great people. In the emerging knowledge economy, the winning organizations will be the ones with the best minds, the most cutting-edge competencies, the greatest imaginations, the fastest reaction time, and the strongest competitive streak—in other words, the one with the *best people*.

POWELL'S RULES FOR RECRUITING AND PROMOTING

But who are these "best people," and how do we find them? Powell advises leaders to hire, place, and promote talented individuals with the following qualities:

> *Look for intelligence and judgment*
> *and, most critically, a capacity*
> *to anticipate, to see around corners.*
> *Also look for loyalty, integrity, a high energy*
> *drive, a balanced ego and the drive*
> *to get things done.*

That sounds a bit like motherhood and apple pie, right? But when you dig down into the way organizations *actually* assess the talents of potential recruits, you find that in many cases, very different screens are put into place. What *actually* happens, more often than not, is that the human resources staff focuses on attributes like length of résumé, number of degrees, and previous job titles.

And, of course, that's not surprising. These are very tangible qualifications. They can be confirmed through reference checks. They make possible (or at least seem to make possible) apples-to-apples comparisons: "Let's see: Joe has managed a staff of 320 people at an oil refinery, whereas Sally has had direct responsibility for 210 customer-service reps in a call center." Also, when one connects the dots on a résumé, one can discern a pattern of career growth, or lack of growth. All this is useful information.

Yet Powell's favorite attributes have none of these advantages. They are intangible and nonlinear. They are hard to infer from a résumé. (Based on these two pages of bullet points, am I confident that this individual can "see around corners"?) But it is precisely those attributes that define the "best" people.

The fact that tracking these attributes is tough only makes that task all the more important. Résumé scanning simply isn't enough. Yes, a broad portfolio of skills and experience can be extremely valuable, but it can also yoke an individual to the past or make that person resistant to change. Skills are hard to acquire, but they become obsolete very easily. Except for jobs that involve truly rare skills or experience bases, therefore, it may be more important to hire a highly talented person with the willingness and ability to learn than someone with a proven (and possibly fixed) skill set.

In other words, you can readily train a bright and willing novice in the fundamentals of your business. It's almost impossible to train someone to have integrity, judgment, intelligence, energy, balance, and the drive to get things done. So good leaders stack the deck in their favor by emphasizing these attributes in the recruitment and promotion phase.

Remember, Powell would never reject individuals who possess critical skills and experience. Only a Stealth bomber pilot can fly a Stealth bomber. Powell *would* insist, though, that in today's chaotic environment, other talents are likely to prove even more important over the long haul, especially when the leader is attempting to develop a high-performance team, or when he is attempting to select and groom future leaders.

Talent is an overused word. Business periodicals talk incessantly about the "war for talent." Executives boldly assert that their companies no longer recruit for skills, they recruit for "talent." (Would that it were so!) But overused or not, it captures the sense of *potential* that is a critical lesson of this chapter. A given individual's talent may be celebrated by all the world, or it may still be latent—just waiting for exploitation by a savvy organization.

With that background, what talents does Powell encourage us to seek out among others? If you review the qualities that Powell endorses in his statement back on page 168, there are at least six specific talents that good leaders look for when hiring, placing, and promoting people. For lack of a better phrase, I call them "Powell's Rules for Picking People." Let's examine each of them in turn.

Intelligence and judgment. When he refers to intelligence, Powell is not referring to I.Q. levels, although I'm sure he'd be happy to have a representation of high-I.Q. individuals on his staff. But the intelligence that adds value to an enterprise may have little or nothing to do with an intelligence test score. Notice that Powell puts "intelligence and judgment" together in one phrase. By so doing, he is emphasizing that in picking people, leaders need to look for the individual who has not only intellectual firepower, but also the experience and common sense needed to bring his or her intelligence to bear on the organizational mission.

The leader has to find people who are bright enough (and, of course, psychologically equipped) to handle complexity—be it complexity in data, people, technology, or ideas. And just as important, the leader has to identify the subset of bright people who are "street smart" and can scope out a situation and decisively choose an appropriate course of action.

In addition, the leader has to identify people whose intelligence translates into inquisitiveness. Not all smart people are hungry for knowledge; in fact, some who have "mastered" a subject are very vulnerable to getting complacent and stuck in the past. Again, we're talking about the intersection of intelligence and judgment. That's where you're most likely to find people who constantly hunger for more knowledge, who seek training and development, who aren't afraid to let go of skills and habits that don't work anymore, and who are always taking the initiative to improve themselves.

A capacity to anticipate, to see around corners. The most successful enterprises are led by individuals who look beyond today, those who are capable of seeing beyond the horizon. These are leaders who grasp emerging shifts in technology, competitors, capital markets, demographics, and consumer needs, and then act on their understanding to launch something new.

In previous chapters, I've referred to Powell's vision of a new, nimbler military—a vision that was realized, and that proved to be a key contributing factor in the Armed Forces' subsequent successes. Most really interesting business success stories have a similar kind of powerful vision behind them.

CNN, for example, grew out of Ted Turner's rigorous scanning of the market's horizon coupled with his intuitive understanding that a 24/7 cable newscast would appeal to a broad base of viewers. (The Big Three television networks could have created a cable news franchise far more easily than Turner, but they failed to see and/or act on what was beyond the "now".)

Other prominent examples of business leaders who showed that they had what it took to look beyond the present include Fred Smith's vision of "absolutely, positively" overnight delivery (FedEx) and Anita Roddick's vision of "boutique" natural-health retailing (Body Shop). What made these visions powerful, rather than outlandish, is that their sponsors really did see around a corner—they paid attention to clues and trends and then acted quickly and imaginatively on their visions of future possibilities.

The peril in reciting a list like the one above is that it overemphasizes the importance of the person at the top. The person at the top can't implement (sometimes can't even develop) the vision on his or her own. Therefore, he or she has to recruit people at all levels of the organization who can look around corners and make sound entrepreneurial judgments based on what they see there. Leaders have to sign up those people who are *eager* to help interpret the storm signs and opportunities on the horizon, and who are just as interested in monitoring the external environment as they are in managing the internal processes of the organization.

Loyalty. Powell has some very clear notions about this key leadership trait. To the people who report to him, he explains loyalty in clear terms:

> *When we are debating an issue, loyalty*
> *means giving me your honest opinion,*
> *whether you think I'll like it or not.*
> *Disagreement, at this state, stimulates me.*
> *But once a decision is made, the debate ends.*

*From that point on, loyalty means executing
the decision as if it were your own.*

Note that Powell does not equate loyalty with obsequious-
ness or ass-kissing. Nor does he equate loyalty with a gate-
keeping mindset—the mentality that says, "I'll shield the boss
from anyone or any data that might make him or her uncomfortable." On the contrary, we've already seen that Powell
looks for the clash of ideas. He expects people to be smart
enough to judge a situation and put forth bright, innovative
input, even if it means arguing with him. Powell's primary
commitment is to *performance* and *mission*, which means that
he tries to surround himself with individuals who are also
committed to larger goals, and who are willing to state their
opinions on how to achieve those goals.

Further, Powell argues that loyalty to the final decision is
also critical. When President Clinton was searching for a
Secretary of Defense, he asked Powell for his opinion on—
among others—Sam Nunn, the Georgia senator with an
acknowledged expertise in military affairs. Powell told
Clinton that while Nunn was a highly qualified candidate, he
might turn out to be too independent to work effectively in
a cabinet setting. As crucial as it is for the president's advisors
to have strong and vocal opinions in their areas of responsibility, it is equally important for them to carry out the president's orders as if they were their own once the final decision
is made.

Again, once the decision is made, debate ends. You take
your best shot at getting the team to adopt your point of
view, but if they don't, you implement with vigor. In other
words, no post-hoc political games, no backstabbing, no lip-
service pretenses, no back-channel dealmaking with others in
the organization in an attempt to undermine the decision.

Your leader and your teammates must be able to rely on you. If they can't count on your loyalty, performance and esprit de corps inevitably suffer.

And if you can't execute the decision as if it were your own, then say so and accept the consequences. You may reasonably ask for the opportunity to gather new information that supports your position, or request to be put on another assignment, or even submit your resignation. (And depending on the circumstances, of course, you may be *asked* for your resignation.) In any of these cases, you have acted with honesty and integrity. Your supervisor and teammates can't fault you for standing on principle. If they are fair, they will be grateful that your loyalty to the larger mission has prevented you from either: (1) sabotaging the mission or (2) lending it only lukewarm support while you nurse your loyalty to your original position.

Integrity. As we have seen in previous chapters, few things matter more to Powell than personal integrity. The message of this chapter, by extension, is never to undervalue integrity when you are recruiting and promoting people for your organization. People with integrity clearly "stand for" something bigger than themselves—a purpose, or a core set of values and ideals—and their actions honestly reflect their convictions. There is a coherence in their decisions and behaviors that reflects their ideals. They are persistent and consistent in how they express their values. They are tenacious in pursuing their purpose.

Let's look at this from the other end of the telescope. A person with a mile-long résumé but only a weak sense of integrity is likely to make expedient decisions. He or she is likely to be focused keenly on organizational politics, or to be driven by what he or she thinks the boss wants to hear, or to be motivated primarily by self-interest. In other words, a lack of integrity is not simply an ethical concern; it also poses a clear threat to the effective functioning of the organization.

This raises the issue of what might be called organizational integrity. This phrase clearly has two distinct connotations. If you expect your organization to conduct itself in an ethical way, then you need to hire people with personal integrity who will set high standards of conduct. And, concurrently, if you want your organization to conduct itself in an integrated way—that is, with structural integrity—this is far more likely to happen if the people you recruit aren't at philosophical cross-purposes with the organization. Leaders build organizational integrity when they pick people who stand for the same purpose, values, and ideals as the team.

When team members share the same purpose, values, and ideals, the "clash of ideas" described in Chapter 2 becomes truly productive because everyone is striving for the same vision and goals. With the common foundation of core purpose, values, and ideals, conflict among team members becomes a healthy path for innovation as they grapple with the best way of getting from here to there.

This concept of fit is so important to Powell that he would be highly unlikely to recruit, retain, or promote someone who did not live the values of the enterprise, regardless of their skills and experiences. Looking to the private sector, Jack Welch was quick to profess that he fired anyone who did not adhere to GE's value system, even if that person's quantitative performance was high. In Welch's opinion, those nonsubscribers threatened the short-term integrity and the long-term health of the company.

When Bill Clinton became president in 1992, he inherited Colin Powell as the chairman of the Joint Chiefs of Staff. It was not a good fit. Powell maintains that on a personal level, he and Clinton actually got along very well. But the Clinton administration tended to use the military in limited ways: for limited objectives, limited air wars, limited humanitarian interventions, and so on. All of this collided directly with Powell's philosophy. The man who formulated the Powell doctrine often found the Clinton foreign policy "amorphous."

Powell had enormous stature at that time, and it appeared that the Clinton administration was inclined to overlook this difference of opinion in order to keep Powell on board. But this "blind eye" had the danger of violating the structural sense of organizational integrity in the Clinton administration. Fortunately for Clinton, Powell had personal integrity, and retired a year later. This enabled Clinton to pick a new chairman, John Shalikashvili, whose philosophy was apparently better aligned with his own. Again, people with integrity not only do the right thing when they take a job, but also do the right thing when they leave a job.

Drive. "I want to try to make things move faster, cut through things more quickly," Powell said in an address to State Department employees. That's drive, and by all accounts, Powell wants to see a lot of it. Powell advises leaders in any organization to pick people who not only have good things in their head and heart, but also have what he calls a "high energy drive" and "the drive to get things done." Don't pick people who passively wait for their marching orders. Don't retain people who whine about pressure, the fast pace of the place, or how hard it is to catch one's breath around this place.

Instead, hire people who live urgency—people who feel that there is not one moment to lose. Promote people who themselves set objectives and priorities beyond their formally assigned goals. Watch patterns of association, and reward those people who seek out people just as driven as themselves as collaborators. (These people are not taking the easy path!) In short, pick people who are impatient with status quo management and are always turning over stones looking for ways to improve things. Driven leaders who surround themselves with driven colleagues are much more likely to achieve extraordinary results.

In fact, Powell takes this philosophy a step further. He believes that good leaders are those who can inspire others to be driven. Therefore, try to pick people for leadership positions who not only are driven themselves, but can inspire others to operate at the same pace. If they can't, don't promote them. At the State Department, Powell has delivered a clear message to people who are interested in career advancement: "Management is a science, leadership is an art, and I will be interested in identifying those people who are leaders, who really know how to turn people on."

Balanced ego. As noted in Chapter 3, Powell doesn't feel that leaders should suppress their strong egos. Likewise, he suggests that leaders pick people who don't apologize for being competent, and don't apologize for seeking high goals. Pick people who are self-assured and who acknowledge their accomplishments when others recognize them.

At the same time, Powell seeks people who aren't overly impressed by their own importance, and who don't take much stock of their press clippings. "To maintain your perspective," advises Powell, "work hard on humility." That's balance. That's the kind of person you want to recruit and promote.

Ego balance implies self-awareness. People who are balanced know when they can blast ahead, and also know when they have to pause, regroup, and enlist new allies with complementary skills. Says Powell:

A good leader surrounds himself with
people who complement his skills.
Only an honest and fair assessment of
your abilities will allow this to happen.

If you're not good at skill X or task Y, either have the humility to go back to "school" and learn what you need to learn, or else team up with someone who can take on those tasks. Towards the twilight of his career at GE, Jack Welch took the startling step of arranging to be mentored about the Internet by very junior (but very Web-savvy) staffers. Now, throughout the corporation, "reverse mentoring" is the rule.

Insecure leaders—a subset of those people with imbalanced egos—can't stomach the idea of working with people who are more skilled than they are. (It's no easier when those skilled people are decades younger, either.) Leaders with the balanced ego that Powell advocates absolutely relish the opportunity to lead the best. As David Glass, the former CEO of Wal-Mart, used to exhort his internal audiences: "Hire people who are better than you are. That's the secret of good leadership."

According to those who have observed him, Powell lives by this principle and seems to enjoy the learning that results. "Powell gives no indication he feels uncomfortable with people who know more than he does," says Marshall Adair, president of the American Foreign Service Association.

SUMMARY

The criteria for hiring, promoting, and placing people—as well as for grooming future leaders—ought to fit the realities of the new world that all leaders face—that is, a world marked by complexity, speed, ambiguity, and constant flux.

Accordingly, Powell advises today's leaders to emphasize intangible attributes like intelligence and judgment, anticipation, loyalty, integrity, drive, and balanced ego when going out in search of talent. The alternative is grim: If you pick people who are weak in these attributes—even if their "tangibles" on the résumé look good—you'll find it very hard to mobilize a team of individuals who take initiative, seek additional learning, show loyalty to each other, share knowledge with each other, and put the team's mission above their own personal needs.

Powell's rules for picking people apply to every level and function of the organization. In fact, the punch line of this entire chapter—one which you've no doubt already figured out—is that these intangible attributes are the very ones that leaders themselves should possess and demonstrate every day. Leaders who follow Powell's rules for themselves and in picking others will make their own lives a lot easier, and they'll be far more likely to achieve success.

POWELL PRINCIPLES

1. **Hire primarily on talent and values, not just on résumés: Résumés, by definition, describe past performance.** In today's environment, they are no longer the best predictors of future performance.

2. **When seeking talent, look for the key Powell traits in hiring and promoting:**

   - Intelligence and judgment
   - A capacity to anticipate, to see around corners
   - Loyalty
   - Integrity

- Drive
- Balanced ego

3. **Seek value alignment.** Don't hire or promote anyone who does not share the same values that drive your organization. Even a talented individual will find it hard to contribute to your mission if his or her values are not in sync with your own.

4. **Hire individuals who are better than you and individuals who can compensate for your weaknesses.** Don't let your ego get in the way. Hire people whom you consider good enough to succeed you, should the situation warrant it. (It's the only way you'll ever be free to move up the ladder, by the way.) Strong leaders are not afraid to surround themselves with people who are better than them.

5. **As a leader, apply these same attributes to yourself.** Hold yourself to the same standards, and role-model them every day. (More on this in Chapter 13.)

CHAPTER 12

TRUST THOSE IN THE TRENCHES

"The people in the field
are closest to the problem,
closest to the situation, therefore
that is where real wisdom is."

IN A WORLD in which unpredictability, complexity, and change are dramatically on the rise, smart leaders understand the importance of "thinking small." They try to cultivate and reinforce a spirit of initiative and leadership among their smaller organizational units. They take the necessary steps to equip these smaller units with the tools, the authority, and the organizational legitimacy that these units need if they are to innovate and move forward quickly. They decentralize, and they keep the clout and authority squarely behind the newly empowered subunits.

Why? Because when things are changing rapidly and the organizational vision is obscured, you have to count on your front-line troops. As Powell puts it, "The commander in the field is always right and the rear echelon is wrong, unless proven otherwise."

It's a quietly radical proposition, because it completely upends the traditional assumptions about power in an organization. And Powell clearly believes that this unorthodox approach applies to *all* organizations. As secretary of state, Powell has asserted that "the real wisdom" lies with his ambassadors, rather than in the Washington bureaucracy. He says, unequivocally, "They're right out there, and we're wrong here until proven otherwise."

According to Barnett Rubin, a political scientist at the Center on International Cooperation, the diplomatic world views Powell's stance as "almost revolutionary." Instead of State Department officials around the world simply serving as eyes and ears for the giant "brain" in Washington, they are now expected to be brains themselves. Invoking a metaphor from the computer world, Powell is advocating a departure from the mainframe in favor of a network of powerful desktop computers, all tightly linked to create an informed, fast-moving, and capable organization.

Why? Because people in the trenches are closer to everything local—conditions, allies, enemies, customers, employees, suppliers, and competitors. They can make decisions and take actions that are faster, more informed, more flexible, and better fitted to local conditions. And this means that they'll make better, smarter, more timely, and more appropriate decisions.

Powell's long-term comrade-in-arms, retired General Norman Schwarzkopf, once echoed this sentiment in more colorful terms: "Even though higher HQ screws it up every way you can possibly screw it up, it is the initiative and valor on the part of small unit leadership that will win for you every time."

In a world as complex, unpredictable and fast moving as ours is, smart leaders try to boost—not inhibit—the initiative and valor of small unit leadership. Among other things, they arm those small units—however far from headquarters they might be—with the right tools, the necessary authority, and the organizational legitimacy. In other words, they decentralize.

Throughout this book, we have discussed the importance of liberating the brains, talents, and imaginations of people. It's been one of the recurring themes which has been presented in a variety of contexts. In this chapter, we cap off the discussion by talking about the importance of organization *structure*, specifically—a structure where formal authority is sufficiently dispersed so that the teams in the field are able to take a primary role in leading the organization's destiny. Once again: decentralization.

THE LESSONS OF THE TWO WARS

To demonstrate the importance of this lesson, one can contrast our national experiences in the Vietnam War and the Gulf War. In previous chapters, I've already noted and discussed one critical difference between these two conflicts: The Gulf War benefited from a clear, well-supported mission, whereas the American involvement in Vietnam did not. But there was at least one other important difference.

In the Vietnam War, a centralized elite—located in the Department of Defense, and specifically within the Pentagon—devised the battle strategy and (to a surprising extent) ran the battles and supporting operations from afar. In his autobiography, Powell notes that Defense Secretary Robert McNamara's detached policies and directives generated counterproductive directives and strange, irrelevant indices of success—for example, says Powell, a village was rated as "secure" when it had a certain number of feet of fence around it "...and a village chief who had not been killed by the Viet Cong in the last three weeks." When Secretary

McNamara announced that every quantitative measurement showed that the U.S. was winning the war, Powell and many other officers in the trenches were astounded at the illusionary thinking. And even though core premises, tactical plans, and metrics emanating out of Washington represented what Powell calls "flabby thinking," the process continued—"all of which we knew was nonsense, even as we did it."

So Vietnam was fought "top down," with little regard being paid to the wisdom of individuals and small units. The Gulf War took a very different course. In fact, one of the main reasons for U.S. success in that conflict was that the Pentagon and the Administration treated the unit leaders "out there" as partners, rather than as subordinates, and allowed them to participate in decision making.

According to retired Major General Perry Smith, the Pentagon, which had been the centralized seat of planning throughout the Vietnam conflict, played primarily a supporting role during the Gulf action. This was in part because leaders like Powell, who had suffered through the mistakes of Vietnam, had resolved that when their time came, they would not repeat those mistakes. In the Gulf War, the meddling and second-guessing that otherwise would have emanated from Virginia and Washington, D.C., were deliberately kept to a minimum.

One might conclude that based on these contrasting experiences and their relative degrees of success, the military might be fully committed to decentralization and "bottom-up" leadership. In fact, the *Wall Street Journal* and other publications have recently reported that there is great internal resistance to significantly changing the way in which the military is organized. Since World War II, for example, the Army has been organized into ten divisions of up to 20,000 troops each. These units are designed to engage similarly large enemy units. Obviously, mobilizing forces on this scale requires enormous coordination and logistical support.

In keeping with Powell's perspectives, suggestions have been made to break up the Army into small, specialized combat units of perhaps 5,000 soldiers each. Under one plan, for example, even the combat units would be specialized—some focused on attack helicopters, others on tanks, and still others on artillery. The goal would be for these units to be light, fleet, and flexible, and to be able to travel anywhere in a matter of days. (This would provide a clear contrast to the weeks or even months that are required to deploy heavy divisions.) Indeed, some proposals suggest shrinking some units even further and significantly expanding the number of small, fluid, Special Forces types of units—as well as very light infantry units—that might well serve as the core of international efforts to combat terrorism and future high-tech wars.

This is a very important point for a simple reason: in the war against terrorism, the enemy is radically decentralized. As described in an earlier chapter, the al-Qaeda "organization" is a loose network of fast, tiny terror cells which can quickly shift from one battlefield to another. They are financed through numerous and diverse decentralized sources, and they operate independently of each other. The question is, are leaders of the U.S. and her allies fighting today's enemy with yesterday's model of military centralization?

It's a valid question, because as discussed earlier, certain camps in the armed forces brass have balked at serious decentralization proposals. The tradition of centralization is often hard to shake. In October and November of 2001, for example, Air Force planes had top Taliban and al-Qaeda members in their cross-hairs at least ten times but were not allowed to fire because they didn't receive clearance from Central Command back in the U.S. until it was too late. The consequence was that ground troops had to begin hunting targets who could have been eliminated from the air earlier in the campaign. In a classic description of the bottlenecks of centralization, *Washington Post* columnist Thomas Ricks wrote:

> *"The core of the clearance problem, as described by several officials, is that the Central Command, which has its headquarters in Tampa, Florida, retained authority to clear attacks on sensitive targets, rather than delegate it to commanders of the air campaign, who were based at Prince Sultan Air Base, located 70 miles southeast of Riyadh in Saudi Arabia."*

As of late November 2001, the frustrations and complaints from the officers in the field were being seriously considered by top brass back in the U.S., but it's clear that policymakers like Powell, who are committed to decentralization and "trusting those in the trenches" continue to have their work cut out for them.

"DECENTRALIZED" DOES NOT MEAN "OPEN SEASON"

Although this chapter has thus far focused on Powell's positions in Vietnam and in the Gulf War, his views on the decentralization of authority have been consistent throughout his career. For example, as commanding officer of V Corps in Europe early in his military career, Powell delivered a clear and surprising message to the commanding officers who reported to him: "I told them that if, as commanders, they found themselves in a fight with my staff, I was predisposed to take their side. The staff existed to serve them."

Many years later, he delivered the same message to State Department employees: "Those of us back here exist not only to support the President, but to support the President's representatives—those ambassadors out there, the missions out there—that are doing the work."

Central headquarters, said Powell in both of these situations, exists to serve the front-line troops. The people at the center are the servants of those under fire, or on the spot. In both cases, though, Powell added an interesting qualification. To the V Corps commanders, he also said, "If, however, I find that any of you are dumping on my people without good cause, you can bet I'll come to their rescue." And to his audience at State, he said, "You are right, and those of us back here at C Street generally are wrong. However, if I find you are wrong, and you are picking on my staff back here, then I will come after you, Mr. Ambassador, Madam Ambassador." No matter how valid the case for any leadership principle—including decentralization—no good leader excuses poor judgments or abuse of personnel under his or her command. Powell's loyalty to his people and to performance remains steadfast.

I suspect that in both cases, Powell was aware that he might be letting the genie out of the bottle. It's not enough simply to announce that you're decentralizing and hope for the best—especially if the troops in the field have spent many years being oppressed by the core. The leader has to explain exactly how the new system will work, and how overriding organizational principles (such as respect for all concerned) will continue to be served. Powell was telling both of his audiences, in effect, that despite the big changes, it would not be "open season" on the newly designated servants at the core.

A second and closely related caveat: Powell is *not* suggesting that top leadership is off the hook—before, during, or after decentralization. They are still primarily responsible for the enterprise's welfare. As implied throughout this book, the leaders must provide the fundamental "rules of the game," including the goal lines (mission, primary objectives, reason for being, fundamental policies, key priorities, and core values) and the sidelines (financial, legal, ethical, and cultural considerations). Top leadership is still responsible for ongoing oversight, and accountable for organizational progress— or the lack thereof. Within this "loose-tight" framework, decentralization works.

Still another caveat pertains to the critical forks in the road, when top leaders clearly must take a more active role in unfolding events. In April 2001, for example, China detained an American spy plane and its crew, and the resulting standoff threatened to escalate into a major international incident. Powell became very involved personally, reviewing all information streams and dictating the strategy and tactics of the diplomacy that eventually resulted in the return to the United States of the plane and its crew.

Presumably, his colleagues at State understood that in such an extraordinary circumstance, the direct involvement of the secretary of state was required. Even so, the evidence suggests Powell took pains to involve his professionals, so that they would give him their best input throughout the unfolding drama.

One risk in putting together a leadership book such as this one is that the subject—in this case, Colin Powell—may wind up sounding like an inevitable success. The recitation of his insights and successes makes it sound as if he was a born leader and simply rose to his proper station in life. In Powell's case, and in just about every other case, this simply isn't true. Leadership skills are *learned*, and wisdom is the result of many years of hard knocks, false starts, and trial and error (this is good news for those of us who want to transform ourselves into more effective leaders).

The topic of decentralization underscores the importance of learning from one's experience. Why does Powell respect those in the trenches? Because he's *been* there. Powell was the first chairman of the Joint Chiefs of Staff to have served on the ground in Vietnam at a rank below that of lieutenant colonel—in other words, low enough to see the world from ground level. He learned, and he remembered his lessons.

According to retired General Mike Lynch, many of the military leaders in the Pentagon don't have the experience necessary to fully understand what they're asking their troops to do. "One of your greatest challenges in the Pentagon," he says, "is trying to explain to other people the problems down at the fighting level. Many of those guys...never had an appreciation of what goes down there at the lowest level. Powell had the advantage of going up through those levels.... When a guy is steeped in the moral and ethical issues down at the fighting level, he's more inclined to back off from gross solutions, and try to equate what they are saying to how difficult it would be to implement it down where he remembers it. Powell was the first chairman who had that experience and was able to carry it up through the ranks."

HISTORY FAVORS DECENTRALIZATION

I'm sure some skeptical readers are still asking: Armies are one thing, but why should there be a leadership imperative to push for decentralization in the private sector? After all, the logic of centralization—consolidate knowledge and power at the top for wisdom, order, and control—seems pretty compelling.

For an answer, start with the fact that history seems to have clearly validated the power of "messy" free enterprise over "orderly" state-controlled economies. Free enterprise depends fundamentally on a foundation of radical decentralization.

Central economic planning was "perfected" by the old Soviet Union, with disastrous results.

The fact is that market efficiencies and market breakthroughs have never sprung forth from the centralized brilliance of any nation's capital, be it Moscow or Washington, D.C. In fact, they usually don't emanate from the centralized brilliance within private sector companies either. No-nonsense decentralization at the corporate level is what's paramount in explaining the economic juggernaut that is the United States. Only rarely—very rarely—have technological and commercial breakthroughs emerged from an organization's formal hierarchical and centralized planning process. Headquarters can support innovation culturally and financially, but it's usually not headquarters that actually comes up with the great innovations and forward leaps—it's the units (the labs, the salesforces, the distribution centers, the little divisions) in the trenches.

The most customer-appealing menu innovations in McDonald's have consistently originated with maverick franchisees. Palm, which launched the mass personal digital assistant craze, started as a small division of 3Com. The e-business solutions strategy that turned IBM around in the late 1990s from a stagnant, rudderless company into the dominant player in the lucrative Internet services arena was not initially a "top-down" strategy. A group of mid-level Internet aficionados within IBM's global payroll banded together as a volunteer guerilla army to conceptualize, develop and eventually "push" the strategy up to CEO Lou Gerstner's attention. Once Gerstner and the top brass got on board, headquarters did something useful. But the genesis and impetus for IBM's current high-growth e-services business—from which Sam Palmisano recently emerged as Gerstner's successor—actually occurred far away from HQ. Most honest leaders in innovative companies will candidly admit that their most fruitful innovations have been hatched in places far from company headquarters.

And by the way, lots of the most interesting innovation happens entirely outside the corporate mainstream. CNN didn't come from CBS, Nike didn't come from U.S. Keds, Starbucks didn't come from General Mills, eBay didn't come from Sotheby's, and Swatch didn't come from Timex. If anything, entrenched companies, far from embracing the innovations that might be their surest path to long-term success, tend to pick legal battles with their upstart competitors.

And when innovators are not sued by entrenched enterprises, it's often only because they've been overlooked or ignored. In the early 1960s, little Celanese came out with polyester tire cords; mighty DuPont's reaction was to invest even more in defending its nylon products. The result? DuPont got smacked, and Celanese racked up a 75 percent market share within five years. Motorola lost billions in revenues and market value to new players like Nokia when it ignored the market's demands for digital technologies for mobile phones, and instead focused on continuously improving its analog base.

The list is endless. Hewlett-Packard ignored Scott McNealy's original business proposal, and the result was an independent Sun Microsystems. Xerox ignored the implications of the technological breakthroughs in its own Palo Alto Research Center. Steve Jobs, who visited PARC, didn't. The result was Apple Computer.

And just to tie together our last two themes (geopolitical trends and entrepreneurship), let me cite Rich Karlgaard, publisher of *Forbes* magazine, who argues that it was the coupling of American decentralization and entrepreneurship that crushed the centralized management of the Soviet Union. An open system fostered a slew of entrepreneurs who created astoundingly successful companies. They included people like Robert Noyce and Gordon Moore (Fairchild Semiconductor and Intel), Bill Gates and Paul Allen (Microsoft), and Steve Jobs and Steve Wozniak (Apple). These passionate individuals—most of whom actually spent time in their garages, or attics, or basements pursuing their vision—ultimately gave the U.S. military and space programs a decisive technological edge, and at the same time overwhelmed the Soviet bloc countries economically.

The point, again, is that nobody "at the top" planned all this. Just as water flows downhill, economic victory goes to the system that is fast, unfettered, and radically imaginative, at the same time that it is fiscally disciplined, brutally lean, and totally accountable. It's called decentralization.

And that's why Powell's lesson is so powerful. An effective enterprise should emulate (and be a part of) an effective market system. Phrased as a question: If centralization didn't work in the Soviet empire, why should it work in a company? If the logic of central planning and execution collapses when it is applied at the country level, isn't there good reason to wonder if it will collapse at the level of an individual corporation? Yes, there will always be a need for the leader who provides the overarching vision, oversight, and, when necessary, the critical intervention—but, as Powell puts it, isn't the commander in the field always right, and the rear echelon wrong, until proven otherwise?

SUPPORTIVE AND LEAN

By his words and deeds, Powell makes the case that no organization can risk the perils associated with detached, too-little-too-late solutions. No organization can afford to maintain a status quo that diminishes people's capacity or willingness to exercise personal initiative. No organization can afford to vest all of its authority and accountability at headquarters.

In the private sector, CEOs like Richard Branson of Virgin, Jack Welch of GE, David Glass of Wal-Mart, Percy Barnevik of Asea Brown Boveri, Ken Iverson of Nucor Steel, and Bob Townsend of Avis would agree. They have understood (and acted on the understanding) that the real dangers of over-centralization go well beyond the cost of salaries and real estate at headquarters. The real problem, as one executive put it to me, is that "the bread and butter is out *there*, but the people making the directives are over *here*."

Accordingly, these leaders and others like them have ensured that their personnel in central headquarters are both *supportive* and *lean*. *Supportive*, in this context, means that they understand that their job is to help the people in the field succeed. *Lean* ensures that the corporate staff can't cost too much or get too meddlesome. Under Barnevik, for exam-ple, fewer than a hundred central corporate staffers worked in the headquarters of ABB, a $30 billion global enterprise. Under Iverson, the rapid growth of Nucor to a billion-dollar enterprise was aided by fewer than twenty-five people at cor-porate headquarters.

Going all the way back to 1962, one finds the decentraliz-ing example of Bob Townsend, who turned Avis around by dramatically pruning the headquarters staff and transforming the company into a thousand little "profit-and-loss" units run by their own managers. The fewer people there were "in here," Townsend reckoned, the less likely it was that they'd inhibit the people "out there" from acting like entrepreneurs. More than any other factor, this was the step that helped turn Avis into a rental-car powerhouse.

In the State Department, of course, Powell does not have that sort of latitude. But he continues to hold his bias toward the "commanders in the field," and whenever possible, he makes a public display of commitment to that bias. As secretary of state, he has eschewed the practice of traveling with a huge entourage on overseas trips. By limiting the size of the group traveling with him, he is forced to rely on the expertise of his people right there in the field. And that's good for him, for the organization, and for them. "The people in the field," he says, "are closest to the problem, closest to the situation, [and] therefore that is where real wisdom is."

SUMMARY

Powell tells us that wisdom resides in the trenches, "unless [it is] proven otherwise." In other words, unless good evidence points to the contrary, the people in the field are capable of running the business, and therefore should do so.

Some readers may protest that some people in the field clearly aren't capable of running a business. That's certainly true. But I'm sure that Powell's advice, in response, would be something along the lines of: So fix those people, or get rid of them. Why structure your entire organization to revolve around them? Start by assuming the best of those who report to you.

In previous chapters, we examined the idea that leaders must possess the ability to build trust among people. Trust is more important than ever before, because it is one of the critical "glues" that bind together people who work in ambiguous, uncertain, even chaotic environments. Unfortunately, though, many discussions about increasing trust in organizations pretty much revolve around interpersonal dimensions— along the lines of, "We must let go of each other's stereotypes," or, "We must learn to communicate with each other more effectively."

These kinds of "micro" interpersonal issues are certainly important, but on their own, they are not enough. William Moody, a recently retired AT&T vice president, told me that toward the end of his lengthy corporate career, he came to realize that trust, or the lack of it, is embedded in the very way we run our enterprises. As he put it, "Either you build systems that unleash trust, or you build systems that diminish trust."

Many of our internal structures, policies, and procedures send the very damaging message that people are fundamentally unworthy of trust. Decentralization, though, works in the opposite direction. Decentralization demands, grows out of, and builds trust. Decentralization compels leaders to trust the people in the trenches, because ultimately, they're the only ones who can win the wars.

POWELL PRINCIPLES

1. **If your division or unit is not decentralized, consider a deep, pervasive, structural and cultural reorganization.** In this fast-paced world, those who are not in constant touch with what is going on in the front lines can't make all the key decisions. Design your organization to take advantage of the intelligence—in both senses of the word—of those who are close to the work and to the customers. Liberate the small units in the field from the suffocating embrace of headquarters and hold them accountable for results.

2. **Use the Internet to make sure that all units and team members have access to information—and to each other.** In Powell's view, all members of the team must have access to key resources. Trusting those in the trenches means trusting them with information. Digital tools are a great help in leveling the knowledge playing field.

3. **Stay on top of key matters.** Decentralization is not an excuse for being out of touch. It is still the leader's responsibility to provide effective leadership. In times of crisis, strong leaders become much more involved—and their troops understand why they are doing so.

4. **Stay lean and supportive.** The people at the core are the *servants* of those in small units in the field. The ranks of those who actually win the wars, or do the business of the company, need to grow much faster than the ranks of those who provide support at headquarters. Larger organizations have to try harder to stay lean and be agile, which again argues for an explicit policy of trusting those in the trenches.

PART III

THE POWELL
CHARACTER

CHAPTER 13

THE POWELL WAY

*"The leader sets an example. Whether in
the Army or in civilian life, the other people
in the organization take their cue from
the leader—not from what the leader says,
but what the leader does."*

WHILE I WAS conducting research for this book, Colin
Powell supplied me with a one-page memo that was
to play a vital role in the book's development. The memo
certainly had an intriguing title: "The Powell Way." And
while the contents of that memo do not constitute a complete road map to Powell's leadership doctrine (as the title of
the memo might suggest), it does provide invaluable insight
into how Powell thinks about the challenges and opportunities of leadership.

Specifically, the memo addresses the challenge of persuad-
ing people to *accept* you as a leader and follow your lead. Why
do people do that? How can the leader enhance his or her
influence and credibility?

INFLUENCE OVER AUTHORITY

Let's begin by examining what Powell thinks *doesn't* work as an enhancer of influence and credibility. When Powell declares that "organization charts and fancy titles count for next to nothing," he provides us with a broad clue. From the leader's point of view, leaning heavily on one's title is a mistake. Paying undue attention to things like status and position won't get the job done. Focusing on the trappings of power and the pull of tradition, or on the fine shadings of an organization chart, is likely to interfere with getting the mission accomplished. At best, the organization goes off in a misguided direction. At worst, it stagnates entirely.

Here's why. Charts and titles are frozen photos trying to cope with an environment that's in constant flux. They're fixed snapshots in a "motion picture" world. If people really followed organization charts and job descriptions to the letter, companies would collapse. Smart leaders tell their people to use common sense, but not to be afraid to bypass and disregard what's codified on the chart if they're pursuing performance excellence. In that spirit, says Powell, he regularly "…told my staff that they should go in and out of my office without exaggerated ceremony."

What this means is that even in well-run organizations led by competent leaders, charts exist. People understand and respect the hierarchy and the departments. But they also freely skirt them in order to get the job done. They access the information they need, talk to the people they need, and collaborate with whom they need.

The same applies to titles. Job titles reflect a reward for prior performance, and they reflect some formal authority— an official status conferring the ability to give orders and induce obedience. Powell admits there are times, like in crisis and battle, where snapping an order might be necessary. But sustained leadership demands much more than authority.

Ultimately, leadership is about power, and power is the capacity to influence, persuade and inspire others. Have you ever noticed that people in organizations will personally commit to certain individuals who on paper possess little authority—but do possess pizzazz, drive, expertise, genuine caring for teammates and products, and a track record of getting things done?

On the flip side, have you noticed that there are people with fancy titles placed in lofty positions on the organization chart, and who inspire nobody? Nonleaders may be formally anointed with all the perks and frills associated with rank, but they have little influence on others, apart from their ability to extract minimal compliance to minimal standards.

All this, I believe, is why Powell asserts that organization charts and fancy titles account for little. He further states:

> *Management is easy. Leadership is*
> *motivating people, turning people on,*
> *getting 110% out of a personal relationship.*

This Powell quote begs the question: What is that inner "stuff" that makes one person a leader and another person not a leader? What are those qualities that enable a leader to get 110 percent out of his or her colleagues?

Some people answer this question by referring to a mysterious factor called "charisma." Powell has often been described as a charismatic leader. But that doesn't give the rest of us much guidance or comfort. Do you have to be born with it? Or are there behaviors that people can study and adopt that will help them exert influence, and *lead*?

Powell would say that the skills of leadership *can* be learned. In fact, he managed to get them onto one sheet of paper.

DECODING THE "POWELL WAY"

As mentioned above, when Powell and I were discussing this question, he gave me a photocopy of a typewritten sheet entitled "The Powell Way." In his opinion, he said, these were the circumstances and attributes that would persuade others to accept your leadership:

- You're a good leader when people follow only out of curiosity.
- They trust you.

  Trust comes from believing in you.

- Competence
- Character
- Courage—moral, physical, mental, spiritual
- Loyalty—up, down, sideways
- Confidence
- Selflessness
- Sacrifice
- Empathy—understand them and their anxieties

Several of these qualities have been discussed in depth in previous chapters. They and the others are worth reconsidering here, as part of our larger effort to decode "The Powell Way."

THE CURIOSITY FACTOR

Powell says that when he was a 21-year-old lieutenant, he learned this bit of wisdom from a tough old sergeant: *People follow out of curiosity.* But what, exactly, does this axiom mean?

By nature, humans are inquisitive animals. Research has shown that when they are confronted with a choice between the "tried, true, and boring" and the "untried and intriguing" (my words), people are more likely to go with the latter than with the former. Evidently, the same rules apply when we choose our leaders. We are more inclined to follow someone who is stimulating, intriguing, and *un*orthodox than someone who comes across as plain vanilla or run-of-the-mill.

There are limits to the amount of stimulation and intrigue that we're willing to put up with, of course. But within those limits, when a leader inspires people to tackle new kinds of issues, consider alternative approaches, aspire to new things, and strike out toward new terrain—and, of course, when that leader *takes the lead* in doing those things—people will tend to follow her or him out of curiosity. Great leaders open up new possibilities for people.

So for leaders and aspiring leaders, here's the prescription: Whet people's curiosity, clear a creative path for them, show them that you yourself are curious—and the chances are good that they'll follow your lead.

THE TRUST FACTOR

"Why would you follow somebody around a corner?" asks Powell. "Or up the hill? Or into a dark room? The reason is trust." Trust is essential for influence and credibility. But how do you build trust? The simple answer is, *Demonstrate the key attributes and personal traits that are likely to build people's confidence in you.* According to Powell, these attributes are competence, character, courage, loyalty, confidence, selflessness, sacrifice, and empathy.

Competence. Obviously, we tend to trust leaders who have skills and experience. But sometimes there's more to this than meets the eye. Many CEOs with years of industry knowledge and company experience have been forced out by impatient boards of directors because their mismanagement got the organization mired in mediocrity or outright failure.

What this means is that competence is multi-faceted. It's more than a reservoir of skills and experience, no matter how deep. Competence also means the ability to learn on a continuing basis (new skills, new businesses), to build harmonious and collaborative relationships (new networks, new resources), and to fire up people's curiosity. If you think about it, these latter competencies described Lou Gerstner, who took over an ailing IBM in 1993 and gradually turned it around, even though at the outset, his technology skills and mainframe experiences were limited.

Character. Leaders with character *stand for something*—a value, an ideal, a cause, a mission. Moreover, leaders with character don't just talk about these things. They exhibit a coherent pattern of behavior that demonstrates what they stand for. In Powell's words, they "figure out what is crucial," and then they "stay focused on it," without allowing side issues to distract them.

I recently asked Monica Luechtefeld, Office Depot's chief of e-commerce, how she was able to lead the charge that ultimately made the Web a core part of Office Depot's total business, from online shopping to supply chain management. "I had to become an evangelist," she replied.

For two years she spent countless hours talking to executives, managers, employees and customers—reassuring, explaining, cajoling, teaching, training. She held seminars, conducted one-on-ones, facilitated the work of engineers who developed systems, worked with salespeople and corporate staff in redesigning jobs, helped change compensation schemes. "I spent nearly 2 years on airplanes," she says, visiting Office Depot personnel and customers around the country. She was relentless on behalf of a cause deemed essential and worthy by the company.

Character is about a leader's daily behavior and decisions being aligned with a mission. It's about walking the talk and rejecting lip service. It's about consistency, clarity, and honesty in words and action. It's about setting the right example and focusing on values.

> *Sometimes I think that I'm probably sounding a little too . . . preachy. But then I realize that all I'm talking about are values, values I was raised with, that you were probably raised with, that are traditional American values. . . . Even if it is corny, it's still valuable.*

Powell also points to his experiences as a parent when he links character and behavior. "Here's a leadership lesson that I've learned from lots of young people, including my own children," he says. "And that is, in leading young people—either as a parent or as a teacher—you can't lecture them as to what they're supposed to do. The way they really learn what the right things to do in life are is by watching. They're not always listening; they're not always paying attention to what you're saying. In fact, they take every opportunity not to pay attention to what you're saying, but they're always watching."

When character is absent, leaders seem to "stand for" whatever seems to be politically or financially expedient, even if their decisions seem fuzzy, contradictory, or self-serving. Powell cites a 1971 Army War College survey administered to senior Army officers who had served in Vietnam. Among other things, says Powell, the report blasted the Army for not confronting its military failures. But the most devastating attack, says Powell, was on the "integrity of the senior leadership. The officers surveyed indicated phony readiness reports, rampant careerism, old-boy assignments, inflated awards, fictitious body counts—the whole façade of illusion and delusion. Their leaders had let them down, and they said so."

How does character generate trust? Because followers believe that the leader believes passionately in something. They believe that he or she will fight for the goals and values that embody that commitment. And finally, they believe that the leader will put tremendous energy into enlisting, encouraging, and protecting others who are willing to walk the same path.

Courage. This is obviously a close corollary to character. For obvious reasons, as a career military man, Powell rates this trait very highly. In any context, though (be it military, public sector, or private sector), leaders should ask themselves the "courage question": *Even if I'm doing things right (operational efficiency, battle readiness), am I doing the right thing? Am I standing for that right thing even in the face of adversity? Am I willing to face risk and loss, and perhaps make significant personal sacrifices, in pursuit of the right thing?*

For Powell, courage—and its sibling, character—is ultimately about one's willingness to take on duty:

> **It is more important to do what is right than
> to do what is personally beneficial.**

Achieving the mission, standing for a value or ideal, setting the right example, walking the talk—these are the foundations of duty. At every opportunity, Powell exhorts leaders to act on principle, even in the face of high personal costs: "Whatever the cost, do what is right!"

Values matter. Integrity matters. Good leaders don't shy from these issues. In a *60 Minutes* television interview, correspondent Ed Bradley asked Powell, "Do you ever think that kids, that adults would perceive you as corny? Do you ever feel that you sound corny?" Powell thought for a moment, and responded:

> *Yeah, I sometimes think that I'm probably sounding a little too corny, a little too preachy. But then I realize that all I'm talking about are values, values I was raised with, that you were probably raised with, that are traditional American values.... Even if it is corny, it's still valuable to hear. It's good stuff.*

Loyalty. For Powell, loyalty is a signpost that points three ways: up, down, and sideways. He also believes, though, that the leader has to take the initiative by demonstrating loyalty to his troops. Powell illustrates this with a personal incident. Bob Woodward's book *The Commanders* came out shortly after the end of the Iraq war. This book, along with a prominent *Washington Post* article on the book, suggested that Powell had been a "reluctant warrior" who did not truly support either the war or his boss, the senior President Bush.

These allegations, which were at best a distortion of Powell's wartime record, threatened to undercut his authority as chairman of the Joint Chiefs of Staff and possibly derail his high prospects within the Bush administration. It was a decisive moment in Powell's professional life: He was exposed, and he needed support.

At that point, President Bush himself stepped forward. He emphatically defended Powell's conduct during the war. He did so publicly and privately, and he made sure that everyone who ought to hear his message did hear it. The fact that Bush and Powell had not always seen eye to eye on all issues only makes the president's strong defense of Powell that much more powerful.

Powell was enormously impressed by this show of loyalty from the commander in chief, who could very easily have left Powell to fend for himself. He didn't forget it. When Democratic bigwig Vernon Jordan asked Powell prior to the 1992 Democratic Convention if he might be interested in being Bill Clinton's running mate, Powell's response was an unequivocal no. Why? There were family and philosophical considerations. But in addition, Powell told Jordan, "George Bush picked me and stuck by me. I could never campaign against him."

Powell speaks often to his own people about loyalty, and his message to them is consistent: *I want you to know you can count on me; I want to know that I can count on you. We may argue about which action to take, but I'll stick by you as we're arguing, as long as you stick by me once a decision is made. No cover-your-butt moves are necessary from you; no knife in the back will come from me.* That's how trust and loyalty become intertwined.

Powell tells a story about an odd episode from his second command in Gelnhausen. In an effort to impress the head of the Pentagon's equal-opportunity program, Powell's mentor, General "Gunfighter" Emerson, ordered Powell to convene his whole battalion to watch and discuss *Brian's Song*, a football movie that had a prominent race relations theme.

But there was a problem: Powell's troops had already seen the movie, and had already discussed it at length. Reluctantly, Powell followed orders and convened the battalion, who dutifully watched the movie for a second time and held a second two-hour discussion of its difficult themes. Both Gunfighter and his visitor went away satisfied, but Powell was deeply embarrassed at having required his men to participate in what was, effectively, a charade—especially a charade on a topic of deep importance.

But when Powell confided these feeling to his sergeant, that subordinate's reply was greatly reassuring. The sergeant told Powell that his men knew that Powell wouldn't have come up with a plan that stupid on his own. They went along with it because they knew he needed their support, and they were happy to demonstrate their loyalty to him.

So it's about loyalty to each other, but it's also about loyalty to the organization. When followers see that a leader is more loyal to the growth and health of the enterprise than to his or her selfish interests, they naturally trust that leader more, and are more open to his or her influence.

Patricia Dunn, global chief executive of Barclays Global Investors (the second largest money manager in the world), tells her aspiring executives that the best thing they can do as leaders is to "think outside themselves." In other words, think how they can be of greatest service to the cause. If you do that, those who also depend on the organization for their livelihood will invest their trust in you because they know that your interests and theirs are congruent.

Confidence. In earlier chapters, we looked at the issue of ego. No one gets and holds a leadership position without a healthy dose of ego. And ego, combined with commitment to mission, is what builds confidence. Sometimes people mistake braggadocio, egomania, and pomposity with confidence. Powell does not believe that self-serving blowhards inspire trust or influence others for any sustained period of time. For Powell, confidence is an issue of *certainty* and *resolve*: certainty in the mission you are trying to accomplish, and resolve in doing whatever it takes tactically to achieve your goals. For

Powell, the leader's ability to feel confidence, and also to convey that confidence to his troops, is absolutely critical for trust building (and ultimately for the performance of the group).

On April 12, 2001, *Time* magazine columnist Tony Karon wrote that "for bringing home 24 Americans from Hainan (China) and helping his boss out of a bind while avoiding turning an incident into a crisis, Secretary of State Colin Powell is our Person of the Week." Karon was referring to an affair in the spring of 2001 that was mentioned in an earlier chapter. In that incident, a Chinese military jet crashed after a midair collision with an American military plane, which then had to make an emergency landing in China. This led to an edgy standoff between the two nations that had the potential to escalate quickly, with grave geopolitical and economic consequences.

"Enter Colin Powell," Karon wrote. "The secretary of state projected infinite cool: unhurried, unfazed, unblinking and even occasionally appearing to enjoy himself." Powell's mission was to create a calm, cooperative atmosphere in which the two sides could help each other out of a mess that neither wanted. This he did with an "unthreatening, business-like approach," whether he was negotiating directly with the Chinese or delegating negotiations to his own team. By projecting an air of quiet competence and steady resolve, Powell was able to calm Americans' jittery nerves and impatience while steadily coaxing the wary Chinese forward. And at the end of the day, when the mission was accomplished, Powell and his team did not immerse themselves in a lot of self-congratulatory hyperbole. "They were given an assignment," Karon noted, "and they completed it, they say. And that's what they're paid to do."

That's a story of *confidence*—confidence that we have the skills to solve this problem, confidence that we can bring along our counterparts on the other side of the table, and confidence that we don't have to toot our horns and apply spin when the mission is accomplished.

Confidence defuses tense situations, as in the Chinese incident just cited. It also heads off (or at least minimizes) the kinds of tensions that naturally arise when an organization tries something new. "When you strike out in a new direction," comments Intel chairman Andy Grove, "in a way you have to feign more confidence than you feel, and you have to be convincing enough and courageous enough that you can affect the rest of the organization to follow you."

Confidence has more than one face. It can be cool, calm, and collected, as *Time* depicted Powell. But it can also be brash, breezy, and bold. During the Gulf War, Powell was cool and collected, while General Norman Schwarzkopf came across as volatile, demanding, and at times explosive. But despite their different personalities, both leaders projected an air of unassailable confidence. Together and separately, they were able to positively influence the troops, the media, and the American public.

Selflessness, sacrifice, and empathy. Let's look at Powell's last three attributes—selflessness, sacrifice, and empathy—as a group. Powell regularly emphasizes how important it is that leaders understand their people's needs, aspirations, and expectations. He stresses *listening* and *caring*. He raises the bar even further by emphasizing the importance of "shared sacrifice":

> *If the troops are cold, you're cold.*
> *But make sure you don't look cold or act*
> *cold. Corporate leaders ought to learn that.*
> *Too often those at high levels don't quite*
> *understand the sacrifices and hardships*
> *of those at the bottom.*

How often have we read about a faltering corporation whose employees face layoffs, salary cuts, higher performance expectations, and fewer resources, while their leaders keep their huge compensation packages and golden parachutes? Certainly, breakdowns in trust can occur when the rank and file conclude that their leaders are incompetent and can't protect their company from competitive pressures. (See "Competence," above.) But *far more damaging* to trust within an organization, in most cases, is a demonstration of unabashed selfishness when others are suffering. Pulling the ripcord on that golden parachute is the final betrayal—but it's very often only the last in a series.

SUMMARY

Powell—in some senses the quintessential organization man—tells us that we can't count on organizational authority alone to get things done. To gain the trust of people and spur them to do great things, leaders can't rely on the formal trappings derived from org charts and job titles. They must *act as leaders.* They must exert influence.

That influence is largely acquired through the modeling of certain key behaviors. "Here's a leadership lesson that I've learned from lots of young people," Powell has said. "You can't lecture them as to what they're supposed to do. The way they really learn what the right things to do in life are is by watching.... They take every opportunity not to pay attention to what you're saying, but they're always watching."

So it's the *behaviors* that count. People who can't act like leaders aren't leaders. By emulating the traits and behaviors encompassed in "The Powell Way," we can equip ourselves to act like real leaders, and in the process, we may even attain that lofty status called charisma.

POWELL PRINCIPLES

1. **Don't be overreliant upon org charts or unduly impressed by job titles.** Respect what's codified, those in authority, but remember that leadership is more about the ability to influence and inspire others.

2. **Curiosity is key.** Curiosity is a key leadership ingredient: The best leaders arouse curiosity. They are interesting and are able to inspire others to act. Boring people stifle curiosity and drive away potential followers.

3. **Always work on building your "trust factor."** The Powell Way is about building others' trust in you. Trust comes from exhibiting many key traits, including competence, character, courage, loyalty, confidence, selflessness, sacrifice, and empathy. Emulate the Powell Way every day.

4. **Walk the talk.** Leaders who talk a good game but do not lead by example will not be respected. Leaders must live by the traits they espouse. Anytime there is a gap between what a leader says and what that leader does, the credibility of that individual will suffer, and sometimes the cost will be too much for the leader (and the organization) to bear.

CHAPTER 14

OPTIMISM IS A "FORCE MULTIPLIER"

*"Don't let adverse facts stand
in the way of a good decision....
Never step on enthusiasm."*

THIS IS A CHAPTER about the power of optimism. It is *not*, however, a rah-rah, "dare-to-be-great," motivational tract. (The world already has enough of those.) Instead, it's an exploration of how good leaders use optimism to help themselves and their organizations achieve extraordinary results.

Powell has made a simple and compelling observation—military in its specifics, but universally applicable—that forms the basis for this lesson: "Perpetual optimism is a force multiplier." By this, he means that a leader's enthusiasm, hopefulness, and confidence multiply as they radiate outward through the organization. Leaders who view the world positively and confidently tend to infuse their people with the same attitude.

In recent decades, one of the great optimists in public life was President Ronald Reagan, who consistently surprised those around him by searching out the positive side of the people he met and the circumstances in which he found himself. This had a considerable impact on the members of the Reagan cabinet, many of whom adopted the same attitude. Even Reagan's secretary of state, George Shultz (who was more often described as "dour" than as cheerful), recognized the importance of Reagan's optimism to his presidency. Shultz also drew a telling comparison between Reagan and the young Powell, saying of Powell that "his upbeat personality was refreshing, and his confident optimism was much like that of Ronald Reagan himself."

So Powell endorses the power of positive thinking as a force multiplier. I think it's fair to say that he would also endorse the converse: Cynicism, doubt, and negativity are "force shrinkers." In other words, leaders who persist in seeing the world negatively are very likely to demoralize, demotivate, and undermine the effectiveness of their colleagues.

I am not suggesting that leaders should stoically accept organizational stupidity, malfeasance or incompetence with a "what, me worry?" smile. Instead, I am stating that good leaders demonstrate a gung-ho attitude that says "we can change things here, we can achieve awesome results, we can be the best." Spare me the grim litany of the pessimistic "realist"; give me the "unrealistic" aspirations of the optimist any day. Ronald Reagan was convinced that the United States could defeat (not merely co-exist with) the old Soviet Union, and his conviction went a long way toward making that outcome happen.

OPTIMISM: "ENTHUSIASM BETWEEN FAILURES"

We are fortunate to have researchers who study optimism. Their research has revealed some important insights for leaders. For example, studies have shown that the roots of optimism lie in the individual's belief that he or she has control over his or her immediate environment. People who believe that they can't influence their environment are more likely to be pessimistic; people who believe that they can are more likely to be optimistic.

But, as Columbia University psychiatrist Susan Vaughan has concluded, "Optimism has little to do with external reality, and everything to do with our ability to regulate our own inner world. It is the *perception of being in control*, not the reality, that really matters."

When people do not believe that they have control, they literally learn to become helpless, according to University of Pennsylvania psychologist Martin Seligman. This "learned helplessness" is a good predictor of passivity, cynicism, and general pessimism. In contrast, optimists believe that what one does matters a great deal, and that is why they take responsibility for their successes and failures. According to Seligman, optimists believe that "the way out is not something that someone is going to bestow on you, it's something you are going to do yourself."

Is that a "realistic" outlook? In a word, no. Consistent with my own research, Seligman suggests that optimists are actually *unrealistic*. They overestimate their skills and their capacity to influence events. Buoyed by their unrealistic view of the world, they show great resiliency in the face of adversity. As Winston Churchill once observed, "Success is measured by your ability to maintain enthusiasm between failures." Meanwhile, under more or less the same conditions, pessimists are giving up. Same circumstances; diametrically opposite outcomes: The only difference is the outlook of the players.

Not surprisingly, Susan Vaughan concludes that optimism is a "desirable distortion of reality." Entrepreneurs and other kinds of change agents understand this conclusion instinctively. They simply shrug off the conventional wisdom about what's possible and what's impossible, and turn a deaf ear when people call them delusional, crazy, or worse. Then they go ahead and attempt the impossible, and they succeed far more often than logic suggests they should. Dr. David Campbell of the Center for Effective Leadership, another scholar who looked at the effects of attitudes on leadership, has concluded that with remarkable consistency, great leaders—ranging from Army officers to business executives—demonstrate enormous optimism.

Obviously, optimism alone is not sufficient to make a great leader. But it's easy to make the case that optimism is a necessary ingredient in the makeup of leadership. Conversely, an overtly pessimistic outlook is likely to derail one's leadership aspirations. As a recent study concluded, "If the aspirant is optimistic, well and good, one can hope he or she may emerge as an effective leader. However, in no case can a pessimist climb the ladder of success."

Why not? "Pessimists," explains Dean Becker, a colleague of Seligman's, "have a way of permeating the atmosphere with dark clouds and ominous forecasts, all of which are hazardous to performance, morale, and teamwork."

On the flip side, there is clear evidence that people resonate with leaders who offer positive messages. This impulse appears to reside somewhere deep in our human wiring. In his book *Learned Optimism*, Seligman examined the presidential elections between 1900 and 1984, and concluded that American voters chose the candidate with the more optimistic message in eighteen out of twenty-two elections. Four-fifths of the time, in other words, voters chose visions of hope and opportunity over visions of doom and gloom. And to the extent that we "vote" in the workplace, investing our trust and hopes in one individual or another, we appear to apply the same standards. We follow the positive leader who can inspire us with hope and confidence.

And optimism also appears to be a self-fulfilling prophecy. "If you build it," as the line in the hit film *Field of Dreams* put it, "they will come." If you don't build it, of course, they *can't* come. Optimism makes things happen. It's a good predictor of career ascent, and it's predictive of excellence in sales, athletics, financial health, and physical health, among other things.

Powell understands and subscribes to the power of optimism. That's why, after coming up with three optimism-rich maxims, he put them under the glass cover on his desk. If his spirit starts to sag, he takes a quick glance at the following:

- It ain't as bad as you think. It will look better in the morning.
- It *can* be done.
- Don't take counsel of your fears or naysayers.

For Powell, the value of optimism is its capacity to spur bold action and extraordinary results. He would not condone what some researchers have called "passive" optimism. Passive optimism is little more than a "don't worry, be happy" attitude. People with passive optimism tell themselves to stay mellow, that everything will work out fine, whatever happens is okay, and others will solve the problems.

In contrast, "dynamic" optimists apply their optimism to attain goals and help others attain goals. They take action. That's the kind of optimism Powell espouses. Don't whine passively about a problem, and don't just smile and shrug it off either. Take responsibility, and do something with the hand you're dealt. "If you get the dirty end of the stick," he says, "sharpen it and turn it into a useful tool."

THE PERVASIVE INFLUENCE OF OPTIMISM

Think about all the things that good leaders need to do (as in the following list) and ask yourself, *Would it be possible to accomplish any of these without a strong dose of optimism?*

- Getting people excited about a new destination and confident about their ability to get there.
- Motivating people to stay up, stay focused, and be innovative during hard times.
- Mobilizing people to commit to big, necessary changes in strategy and organization, during either good times or bad times.
- Helping people *see* and *believe in* new possibilities.
- Getting people to overcome both external hurdles and internal obstacles in pursuit of bold goals.

Success, as Thomas Edison is reputed to have said, is 20 percent inspiration and 80 percent perspiration. (He would know, having tried literally thousands of materials before finding one that could serve as a filament in a light bulb.) If that's indeed true, then optimism has to play a critical role in the success equation. Optimism prepares the ground for inspiration, by enabling you to take up a challenge that has defeated others before you. (*There must be a way to use electricity to illuminate a room!*) And then optimism plays an even more important role, by getting you and your colleagues back into the lab day after day, week after week, ignoring the growing mound of failures and looking forward confidently to ultimate success.

GROUNDED OPTIMISM

Leaders who use their positive outlooks to enhance their chances of success demonstrate what I would call "grounded optimism." Here's what they do:

1. **Good leaders make optimism an organizational priority.** People become more optimistic if three conditions exist. First, they are informed and involved. Second, they feel that they have the power and authority to take action. Third, they are committed to a compelling direction and an inspiring vision.

   Accordingly, good leaders do three things. First, they communicate clearly and consistently the problems and challenges the organization is facing, as well as possible solutions, positive news, and exciting possibilities. They solicit people's input and help. Second, they empower people by giving them the authority and the tools to get things done. Third, they make sure that people are excited and inspired by the mission.

2. **Good leaders stoke the fires of optimism.** Powell recalls a time when his troops got excited about the possibility of winning the division boxing championship in the brigade sports competition. They were bubbling over with ideas and initiatives. "I told them to go ahead," he recalls. "Never step on enthusiasm."

   That's good advice. Optimism includes an "I can do that!" enthusiasm. Effective leaders encourage that attitude and, whenever possible, help focus it on the unit's mission.

   It goes deeper than that, however. Powell says: "Don't let adverse facts stand in the way of a good decision." Maybe that struck you as a very curious statement when you first encountered it at the beginning of this chapter. After all, haven't we learned in previous chapters that Powell aggressively seeks out the truth and treasures the illuminating detail? Is he going against his own advice here?

   Not really. Powell is simply reminding us that a great mission, fueled by optimism, can overwhelm some troubling data. Sure, a handful of sugar in the gas tank will stop the vehicle in its tracks, but some sand on the axles won't. Entrepreneurs and other change agents *assume* that their paths will be littered with facts that suggest that their goals are unreasonable, if not impossible. That's where passion comes in.

Optimistic leaders are so committed to their vision that they do absorb the facts—both "good news" and "bad news"—that will ultimately help them achieve their goals. At the same time, they often choose to reject "facts" that tell them they can't succeed. Philippe Villers, an entrepreneur who has launched a number of start-up businesses, has defined entrepreneurship as "unreasonable conviction based on inadequate evidence." That's passion. Leaders stoke it.

Does this sound irrational, even delusional? Well, try it on for size. Many leaders before you have done so, to great effect. "You can't proceed in a calm, rational manner," Jack Welch told the *Wall Street Journal.* "You've got to be on the lunatic fringe." And as Oracle CEO Larry Ellison told *Forbes* magazine, "When everyone says you're crazy, that's exactly where you want to be." Optimism that borders on passion—even mania—seems to be a solid leadership tool.

John Doerr, one of Silicon Valley's most respected venture capitalists, says that any competent venture capitalist looks for a climate of passion in the start-ups that he or she decides to invest in. The new venture simply can't survive on money alone. There are simply too many obstacles out there (all those adverse "facts") waiting to derail that start-up. Passion is the fuel that keeps the uphill momentum, and passion is fueled and sustained by optimism.

3. **Good leaders stay disciplined and in touch while pursuing extraordinary goals.** I noted previously that while entrepreneurs and change agents let negativity roll off

their backs, they don't ignore practical problems and challenges. Instead, they confront them. As disciplined optimists, they stay in close touch with their environment: *What do we have to be optimistic about today?*

Disciplined optimism means four things. First, it means *substantial, continuing investment* in things like mission, people, details, looking below the surface, challenging the pros, and many of the other topics covered in this book.

Second, it means *fine-tuning one's optimism* in light of the situation. Martin Seligman notes that if the cost of failure is high —"such as getting into an affair which will lead to divorce if your spouse finds out, or as a pilot, having another drink at a party before a flight"—good leaders temper and adjust their optimism. Blind optimism is silly. Informed optimism is an indispensable foundation.

Third, disciplined optimism means *pursuing a mission and goals that people truly believe to be achievable*. Good leaders set extraordinary, even "insane" goals. They know it doesn't matter if outsiders say you're crazy as long as you and your team believe that it can be done. On the other hand, warns Seligman, setting truly unattainable goals is a form of naïve optimism. Employees soon become disgruntled and cynical when they realize that the rhetoric doesn't match reality.

Fourth, disciplined optimism involves *tracking progress*. Good leaders monitor efforts, post data, discuss results, and adjust their sights accordingly. When people are in the dark as to where they and the organization stand, optimism can't take root and flourish.

Powell has applied this principle throughout his career, as can be seen with the America's Promise foundation that he launched after his retirement from the military. The foundation tracks its progress against five specific metrics:

providing at-risk youth with an adult mentor, a safe place to go after school, a healthy start, a marketable skill, and a chance to serve others. On the foundation's Web site is a detailed "report card" summarizing the foundation's progress, including the number of volunteer man-hours, after-school programs, educational scholarships, and youth impacted per corporate partner. Powell even persuaded PricewaterhouseCoopers to "audit" the foundation's efforts, in effect turning the qualitative into the quantitative.

Why all this tracking and monitoring? Well, one of the best sources of optimism about the future is a solid track record. By setting goals and measuring progress (and, of course, by *making* progress!), Powell sets the stage for more success in the future. When he exudes optimism, his internal and external constituents understand that his optimism is well founded.

In a 2000 interview, for example, Powell pointed to the foundation's accomplishments in achieving its five-point mission. He then looked forward. "I'm confident of victory," he said simply. And those who were tracking the foundation's progress along with him understood and shared his optimism.

It's a virtuous cycle. Optimism encourages people to embrace impossible tasks, and success at those tasks (tracked, assessed, and discussed) positions the leader to set even higher standards for the future. "Our philosophy," says Powell, "is that you only get back what you expect, and, if you start low, you'll end low. So we start high. We have the highest expectations and it rarely fails."

4. **Good leaders teach optimism.** The research suggests that many of us did not have the good fortune to have been raised with an attitude of optimism. It appears that Powell was one of those lucky few. He refers to his father

as "the eternal optimist," and makes it clear that he is grateful for this legacy from his father.

Does that mean that the rest of us are out of luck? I don't think so. If Powell learned optimism from his father, optimism is something that can be learned—and taught. In fact, says David Campbell, "It's the role of the manager/leader in the twenty-first century to teach optimism."

I don't think Campbell is advocating either cheerleading sessions or seminars in optimism research. Instead, I think he means that good leaders teach people how to interpret difficult situations more positively. They teach them how to handle adverse facts, and how to calibrate for the counsel of naysayers. They teach them the value of holding "unreasonable convictions." They teach them how to bring positive thinking to bear on their work in creative and realistic ways.

5. **Good leaders model optimism.** By and large, people want to believe. They look to leaders for inspiration. They look to leaders for optimistic cues, patterns of upbeat behavior, and confidence about the future of the organization, especially when criticisms and obstacles are hurled their way.

OPTIMISM MEETS REALITY

"I'm a very optimistic person about the world we live in," Powell said two years ago to an interviewer from India when he was secretary of state–designate. "There are still our Iraqs and our Irans and our Libyas. None of these rises to the level of the Cold War. None of these threatens our lives."

Since that time, "adverse facts" have presented themselves in spades. Terrorists killed over 4,000 people in New York City, Washington D.C., and Pennsylvania. Mysterious outbreaks of anthrax set the nation on edge. A global war on terrorism took the form of specific military actions, which (like most military actions) divided the world into supporters and opponents. Meanwhile, the stock market and the larger economy swooned. The longest economic boom in American history came to an end.

So was Powell's optimism misplaced? Not at all. First of all, history is replete with ups and downs. Secondly, remember that optimism has little to do with external reality and everything to do with our perception of what we can do with it. According to senior *New York Times* columnist Bill Keller, Powell sees a "fresh sense of opportunity" in the post-September 11 world: liquidating a long-festering growth of clandestine terrorism networks, creating a sense of global trust and common purpose among hitherto competing or hostile nations, and even resolving some intractable conflicts in the Mideast and beyond. Keller also notes that "one man who...talks about the world with the same tone of bright promise (as Powell does), is President Bush," so there is every reason to believe that even in these troubling times, optimism will serve as a force multiplier.

As corporate leaders set out to deal with their own long list of post-Sept. 11 challenges, they would be wise to emulate and draw upon Powell's optimism. Consumers, investors, and employees alike will be looking to them to show imagination, resiliency, discipline, and passion in their own sphere of influence. The early trends are encouraging.

The bigger the challenge, the more useful a tool optimism is likely to be. Great leaders inspire a sense of hope, possibility, and confidence, even under the most trying circumstances. That is why they are needed so badly, and why their optimism is, indeed, a force multiplier.

SUMMARY

Optimism helps both individuals and organizations. It helps them start dreaming, realize their dreams, and dream bigger dreams.

Optimism, as we've seen, helps build thick skin and perseverance. No leader—and certainly not Powell—is immune from attack. When the attack comes, a thick skin is a great shield. When Powell's name was first floated as a potential secretary of state, left-leaning critics castigated him for being too aggressive, while those on the right faulted him for being too cautious. "I have a cottage industry of critics," Powell said good-naturedly. Every good leader does.

Organizations benefit when they see their leaders shrugging off the criticisms and moving forward optimistically. Optimism, especially optimism reinforced by a track record of performance, builds confidence. Conversely, cynicism and pessimism tend to dampen and deflate an organization.

Optimism becomes even more important in times of uncertainty or during a sweeping change effort. It helps keep people motivated, focused, and innovative when the organization most needs those qualities. It helps individuals overcome obstacles and circumvent bureaucracies that might otherwise defeat them.

Strong leaders make optimism a top priority. Within reason (and without departing from reality) they reject the "adverse facts" that tell them they cannot succeed. They understand that, as Churchill said, success is measured by our ability to maintain enthusiasm between failures.

POWELL PRINCIPLES

1. **Put optimism on your desktop.** Powell tells himself, and us, that "it ain't as bad as you think. Things will look better in the morning."

2. **Don't take counsel of your fears or your naysayers.** Again, don't let naysayers or partial facts tell you that it can't be done. Remember, positive distortions of reality can be highly desirable.

3. **Make optimism a top priority.** While most leaders do not have such a "soft" value at the top of their to-do list, they should. Research shows that optimism and attitude can make a huge difference in a team's ability to accomplish its mission.

4. **Spread optimism around the organization.** In addition to living optimism, it is the leader's responsibility to make sure that others follow suit. Both pessimism and optimism can be contagious. It is the leader who sets the tone, and he or she must be sure that optimism, not pessimism, permeates the fabric of the organization.

5. **Make optimism the fuel for bold and disciplined action.** Optimism is not just rah-rah cheerleading. Its real value is in spurring concrete decisions and behaviors that help us develop creative paths to achieve exceptional goals.

CHAPTER 15

TAKE LEAVE WHEN YOU'VE EARNED IT

"Never become so consumed by your career
that nothing is left that belongs
only to you and your family.
Don't allow your profession to
become the whole of your existence."

THE MESSAGE OF THIS chapter may surprise you. Prior chapters have emphasized more hard-hitting aspects of leadership—activities like creating a compelling mission, invoking high and nonnegotiable standards, attending to details, mobilizing the troops, taking action even without permission, digging below the surface, and so on.

But there's another side to Powell. He and a Soviet general, Mikhail Moiseyev, were making a joint ceremonial tour of a warship. When they got to the ship's galley, they found what they felt constituted the makings of a new bilateral competition: a sack of potatoes and some potato peelers. The question was posed: Who could peel a potato faster? So the short-lived "spud war" broke out—and was promptly won by Moiseyev.

What's the point of the story? I think it illustrates an unexpectedly playful side to our otherwise sober main character. But it also hints at a central piece of his leadership philosophy: the need for balance. Consider the following four pieces of advice that Powell has consistently given to his direct reports over the years:

- Have fun in your command.
- Don't always run at a breakneck pace.
- Take leave when you've earned it.
- Spend time with your families.

THE LESSON OF BALANCE

What does this have to do with leadership? As it turns out, a great deal. *Balance* is a term that Powell has used frequently when describing leadership, so we need to understand what he means when he invokes it.

We instinctively know what balance is—or, perhaps more accurately, what it isn't—because we've all seen *imbalanced* managers during our careers. For example, there's the loose, casual guy who is big on making sure that everyone feels good. There are plenty of good times and backslapping when he's around, but after a while, it becomes clear that this engaging character lacks *balance*. He keeps putting off the serious work—like fixing a big systems problem, addressing a major customer complaint, or confronting a sticky personnel problem—because he knows it has the potential to be difficult, or unpleasant, or risky.

Most of us have also seen a lack of balance at the other end of the spectrum. We've run into the intense workaholic who logs mind-numbing numbers of hours chained to her desk—but at the same time demonstrates little understanding of or empathy for her coworkers. She has become one with her PC and her spreadsheets.

Then there's the manager who tenaciously defends the status quo. "This is the way we've always done it," he says, "so this is the way we're going to keep on doing it." In this case, the lack of balance takes the form of rigidity. Sometimes this rigidity take a disguised form—for example, it may be wrapped in lots of "yeah, but" objections, excuses as to why he can't learn a new way of doing things, an intolerance of people who don't act like "they're supposed to," and so on. Either way, it's a case of imbalance.

And of course, there's the person who has been promoted to a general management position because she was an outstanding technical specialist. She was great at running debugging and documentation teams, but now she's on unfamiliar ground. (Senior management hasn't given her new skills; it's simply moved her up the ladder.) Her imbalance of skills makes it difficult for her to grasp the big picture, articulate a vision, or get others to sign on to that vision.

These are all *imbalanced* people. They're one-dimensional. In a constantly changing and uncertain world, they're stuck with a limited tool kit—with a fixed repertoire of skills and habits. If you don't actually have to work for them, it's easy to feel some sympathy for them.

BALANCING WORK AND FAMILY

I find it notable that in Powell's first major introductory speech to State Department personnel, his strong comments about performance and mission were complemented—and counterbalanced—by an interesting aside:

> *I am 63 going on 64. I don't have to prove to*
> *anybody that I can work 16 hours a day if I*
> *can get it done in eight. If I'm looking for you*
> *at 7:30 at night, 8:00 at night, and you are*
> *not in your office, I will consider you to be a*
> *very, very wise person. (Laughter). If I need*
> *you, I will find you at home. Anybody who is*
> *logging hours to impress me, you are wasting*
> *your time. (Laughter and applause).*

Powell then went on to talk about the importance of *having a life*. He spoke, too, of the importance of spending time with loved ones:

> *Do your work, and then go home to*
> *your families, go to your soccer games.*
> *Unless the mission demands it, I have*
> *no intention of being here on Saturday*
> *and Sunday. Do what you have to*
> *do to get the job done, but don't think*
> *that I am clocking anybody to see where*
> *you are on any particular hour of the day*
> *or day of the week. We are all professionals*
> *here and can take care of that.*

Yes, there are likely to be times when you'll be on the road and unable to attend your kid's soccer game. There may well be stretches of time when you're putting in fourteen hours a day at the office, or giving up weekends, or conforming to some other kind of grueling, imbalanced schedule—when the mission demands it, as Powell would put it. (Undoubtedly, Powell has frequently found himself in that space since Sept. 11, because the mission *does* demand it.)

But these have to be the imbalanced exceptions to the balanced rule. Why? In part because no organization that counts on burning up its people is sustainable. People eventually rebel against, or get broken down by, that kind of structural abuse. Furthermore, the organization puts itself at risk if it puts key decisions in the hands of individuals who are suffering from physical, mental, or emotional burnout. Leaders (at every level in the organization) have to stay sharp, focused, imaginative, and inspired—which they're unlikely to do if they're being tormented by their organization's insatiable demand for them.

Today, Americans are working more and vacationing less. Employees in the United States spend significantly more hours on the job than employees in Australia, Canada, Japan, Brazil, Great Britain, or Germany. While this "living to work" philosophy (a term coined by the University of Chicago's Richard Freeman) has resulted in unparalleled wealth and productivity, it has also created extraordinary stresses and tensions in people's lives.

In fact, the "living to work/working to live" question (a question of balance) has become a major issue among managers and white-collar employees alike. For years, observers have cited the common complaint of many managers that they simply don't have sufficient time to enjoy their family. This is likely to become an issue of worldwide importance, because an increasing number of countries around the world seem to be gravitating towards the American "living to work" model. Meanwhile, in the United States, recent research suggests that employees are beginning to value time as much as money.

Powell is not a philosopher, and therefore he tends to weigh in little on such topics as what makes life meaningful. However, leaders who do not buffer themselves and their people from the pressure to work constantly, he feels, cannot remain effective in the long haul. He certainly has paid careful attention to his own career progress. All well and good, he says—but not enough. "Never become so consumed by your career," he advises his subordinates, "that nothing is left that belongs only to you and your family. Don't allow your profession to become the whole of your existence."

Powell further advises leaders to extend this same philosophy to those for whom they are responsible: "As a leader, you need to recognize that people need balance in their lives, have outside interests, have families and need to spend time with them. Unless absolutely unavoidable, you should not infringe on off-duty time."

Many managers are skeptical of this philosophy. They equate it with "coddling." Their viewpoint is often counterproductive, however, for studies show that employees who aren't overtired or overstressed make better decisions, stay with a company longer, and avoid the physical and mental consequences of burnout.

Hence, if you're equating the quality of performance with the quantity of time on the job, think again. Change the way you and your colleagues allocate your hours. Don't expect someone down the line to make up the slack for your missed deadlines. Build realism into schedules and workloads. Urge people to get adequate rest and relaxation. Make vacations sacrosanct, unless the mission absolutely demands a contribution from the vacationing individual. Identify sources of unnecessary stress in the workplace, and work to minimize them. (People will tell you if you ask them.) Conversely, identify sources of satisfaction and inspiration in the workplace, and reinforce them. Remember that sometimes less (as in stress, busywork and time on the job) is more (as in unit performance, morale, and innovation).

FUN: A MUST FOR
PERFORMANCE AND INNOVATION

Not content with advising us to "get a life," Powell pushes us further by advising us to *enjoy ourselves* and *have fun while we're working*. If you're not having fun, either you're in the wrong line of work, or you're doing your job wrong. He recently told an interviewer that toward the end of the Foreign Services Institute (FSI) course—a crash course for newly appointed U.S. ambassadors, in which Powell participates—he gave his distinguished students an important bit of instruction:

> *On the last day of the FSI course, I spoke to the ambassadors and told them to take seriously their role as the President's personal representatives. At the same time, I encouraged them to have great fun in their new assignments. Fortunately, the two are not mutually exclusive.*

Not mutually exclusive? I've been in workplaces where that certainly didn't seem to be the case—places where the general air of propriety and decorum verged on grimness. In many chronically stuffy settings, even the introduction of "casual Fridays" has proven to be a truly insurrectionary development.

I don't mean to overstate the importance of a dress code. But anyone who has successfully executed a start-up, a spin-off, or any major organizational change effort knows that achieving success against long odds requires a heap of enthusiasm, excitement, zest, and even joy. In short, it presupposes the ability to have fun. If formal business attire opens the door to fun, then so be it. The point is to *set the table for fun*.

In my studies of successful leaders like Sun Microsystems' Scott McNealy, Blue Cross/Blue Shield's Ed Sellers, the

Body Shop's Anita Roddick, and Virgin Atlantic's Richard Branson, I found several consistent themes. First, of course, they all take their work and responsibilities *very seriously indeed*. You don't get to the top of a company, and then take that company to the top of its industry, without taking care of business. At the same time, they all view fun in the workplace as essential to innovation, risk taking, team spirit, and performance.

Accordingly, they take fun seriously. In their organizations, fun has emerged as a business priority, and encouraging employees to "work hard and play hard" is an informal but powerful corporate value. For these leaders, fun takes the form of formal structures like on-site fitness centers, parties, and celebrations. But, even more important, it is also ingrained in the work itself, and in the working relationships. When people have fun together, as these leaders see it, they are far more likely to accomplish extraordinary things together.

One of the best predictors of a company's health is how much fun people are having as they are working their butts off. Conversely, one of the best predictors of lower innovation and higher personnel turnover—and which ultimately leads to corporate disease and demise—is when you start hearing the talented people say, "It's just not *fun* anymore." I don't care how big the enterprise has become, or how grand its plans are: If there's no joy and delight in the organization, all bets are off.

The leader sets the stage for this environment by being a good role model. Throughout his career Powell has reminded people to enjoy themselves at work and *not* to mistake his "easygoing style with lax standards." He has also shown that enjoying oneself includes finding fun in the unexpected. In particular, he has demonstrated that humor is a wonderful tool to relieve tension and puncture stuffiness and pomposity. It is also a behavior that others are quick to imitate.

Powell frequently seasons his personal interactions with humor, including self-deprecating humor. On his first visit to George W. Bush's ranch after the 2000 election, he was well aware that the reporters on the scene were hanging on to his every word, hoping that the secretary of state–designate would give them a scoop—or perhaps make a newsworthy blunder. "I'm from the South Bronx," Powell finally said in his best military deadpan, "and I don't care what you say. Those cows look dangerous!"

Early in Powell's tenure at State, the Bush staffers sent out some well-intentioned but bureaucratic directives about the importance of people turning off their cell phone ringers during meetings. Powell dutifully passed along the directives, then went off on a trip to Florida. When he opened his first key management meeting after this trip, he pulled out a garish pink and white conch shell and held it up to his ear. "Shell phone," he explained impishly.

During a nationally televised news conference on September 13, 2001, when the tension was palpable and everyone's nerves were on edge, Powell showed his style again in an interaction with a correspondent during the question-and-answer period:

Reporter: "Are you going to ask Pakistan to put their money where their mouth is?"

Powell: "I wouldn't put it so crudely, Andrea."

Reporter: "I'm not a diplomat."

Powell: "Some say I'm not either."

That little comment generated a wave of relieved laughter which helped dissipate some of the tension in the room—and maybe even in the country.

"OK, cute," you may be saying, "but what do funny little quips have to do with leadership?" I think I'll let Herb Kelleher, the recently retired CEO of Southwest Air, answer that one. During his long tenure at the helm of Southwest, Kelleher was labeled the best CEO in America by several publications. By almost any measure, his track record was exemplary. For example, Southwest is the only U.S. airline to have consistently turned a profit over each of the past twenty-eight years. It has achieved a market capitalization that dwarfs that of many better-known competitors.

There are many technical factors that contribute to Southwest's economic success, including a sophisticated system of point-to-point flights and rigorous cost controls. But if you ask Kelleher, he'll tell you that it's the *people* who make the difference. And he'll go on to say that a sense of humor is so important for working at Southwest that it has become a key selection criterion, especially for would-be leaders.

Kelleher certainly lived up to the standard. He became celebrated for antics like popping out of overhead compartments into the arms of unsuspecting travelers, dressing up as Elvis for an investors' meeting, and driving a motorcycle into the first floor of Southwest's offices to address employees. When Southwest became embroiled in a trademark controversy with a regional airline, Kelleher challenged the CEO of that airline to a winner-take-all arm-wrestling contest for the rights to the phrase in question. The challenge was accepted, and the two CEOs met for battle in a very convincing send-up of a World Wrestling Federation event.

I feel that I should report on the outcome of the contest. Kelleher lost, but because of the shenanigans, he quickly worked out an amicable deal with the other CEO, and in the process generated huge amounts of fun for his troops. Further, as he pointed out, he significantly cut down on his legal bills.

In today's fast-paced, fingernail-biting competitive environment, a leader who doesn't have a good sense of humor will probably not be effective in the long run. The grim, dour "professional manager" doesn't cut it anymore. Leaders who want to inspire imagination, exuberance, and passion in their workforce need to inject the yeast of humor into their organizations. There's no one right style. Powell's dry reserved sense of humor is certainly different from Kelleher's, but it's just as effective. Find your own style, and use it.

Most of all, don't just talk about fun; *have fun* in your command. Powell is so adamant about this point that he even tells leaders to surround themselves with people who show joy at work. "I like staff members who take their work seriously, but not themselves. I like people who work hard and play hard."

In other words, leaders would be wise to seek people who themselves have a balanced outlook on life—people who are very committed to their work but who are also just plain fun to collaborate with, who like to laugh a lot (especially at themselves) and who have some non-job priorities which they approach with the same avid interest and curiosity that they do their work. Powell would be the first to reassure you that such actions pay off.

SUMMARY

This chapter gives us two key suggestions about a leader's outlook on life. First, he says, remember that in the long haul, the balanced leader will beat the grim workaholic, the one-dimensional ideologue, the self-important blowhard who takes himself oh-so-seriously, the stern and somber hierarchy climber, and the ultra-earnest "I'm a professional." Not just once in a while—*every time.*

Second, if you're serious about building more balance into your life, start *acting* more balanced by using the techniques described in this chapter.

If you enjoy yourself, people will notice. Even as he was working day and night in the spring of 2001 to resolve the downed-plane standoff with China (a confrontation that had the potential to spiral up into truly dangerous territory) Powell appeared relaxed and calm, and had a ready smile. *Time* correspondent Tony Karon noted that "the secretary of state...[appeared] to enjoy himself." I'm sure he did—because for Powell, enjoying oneself is a personal and organizational priority.

Life is too short to allow for too much grimness. Take leave when you've earned it. We're all "serving our last command," Powell says in his elliptical way. Help yourself, and help your organization, by having fun and making fun for others.

POWELL PRINCIPLES

1. **Strive for balance.** Powell is unequivocal here. Don't neglect home and family life. Go to those Little League games and that piano recital. Don't spend yourself entirely at work. If your workplace gets jealous, think about a change. Again, life is short.

2. **Have fun in your command.** Research suggests that those who have fun in their jobs perform better, innovate on a more consistent basis, and are less likely to crack under pressure.

3. **Don't clock hours for hours' sake.** Don't confuse activity with productivity. Powell is not necessarily impressed by those members of his team who work long hours. (It's the productivity, at the end of those hours, that counts.) Get things done, take your vacations, and encourage others to do the same.

4. **Make it a priority to create a balanced, fun environment for others.** Remember, an environment where people work hard, play hard, and take leave when they've earned it is the optimal environment for morale, innovation, and performance.

CHAPTER 16

PREPARE FOR
LONELINESS

~~~~~~~~~~~~~~~~~~~~

"Command is lonely."

G REAT LEADERS ARE rarely alone. All the evidence suggests, however, that they are often lonely. This chapter explores that paradoxical reality and, drawing on Colin Powell's experience, suggests ways in which leaders should think about their relationships with other people.

"The President," notes historian Paul Johnson, "is a lonely man in times of crisis." Take a recent example: the terrorist attacks on the World Trade Center and the Pentagon on September 11, 2001. On that day, and in the anxiety-filled days and weeks that followed, George W. Bush was a lonely man. He didn't lack for company, I'm sure—advisors, cabinet members, diplomats, military people, members of Congress, and family members, among others—and I'm sure he got plenty of phone calls, faxes, notes, e-mails, and other communications.

Nevertheless, somewhere in that difficult period, I'm sure he felt very much alone. "It's lonely at the top," as the saying goes. But why? Because the enormous weight of the presidency was on his shoulders, and that weight simply couldn't be shared with or laid off on anyone else. "The buck stops here," as President Truman used to say. The American public, as well as our allies around the world, looked to Bush for hope, inspiration, and wisdom—and Bush, alone, had to deliver.

Fortunately, serving as the President of the United States in a moment of deep national crisis is the most extreme case imaginable. Most of the rest of us, whether we head up teams, departments, divisions, or even whole corporations, will never face a situation that is even remotely comparable. The world will not end if we make a bad call. Even so, a sense of aloneness is endemic to leadership at any level in any enterprise. It is something that great leaders learn to accept, work with, and even use to their advantage.

TAKING FINAL RESPONSIBILITY IS LONELY

"Command is lonely" declares Powell, and this simple assertion forms the basis of this chapter. At the end of the day, says Powell, after a leader has listened, collaborated, delegated, and empowered, it's time for him or her—and nobody else—to make the decisive and critical decisions. It's time to set the right course of action, inspire hope and confidence, bless the right initiatives, anoint the right people, articulate the right standards, and define the right metrics. In other words, it's time to show true leadership. Your decisions may reflect input from many people, but they're *your* actions. And whatever the aftermath of those decisions may be, *you own it*.

Most people don't get enormous responsibility thrust upon them suddenly. Most leaders work their way up some kind of ladder, acquiring increasing degrees of authority and responsibility along the way. At some point along that path, most aspiring leaders grapple with (or at least *ought* to grapple with) some very tough questions: Can I bear the final responsibility? Can I take the heat, when it comes? Can I stand alone?

In a military context, with lives at stake, these questions take on a special urgency. In his autobiography, Powell describes the development of the plan—code-named Blue Spoon (later renamed Just Cause)—to invade Panama and take out the erratic dictator Manuel Noriega in December 1989. After a series of serious developments in Panama, culminating in the killing of Marine Lieutenant Robert Paz by Panama Defense Forces, Powell, who was then chairman of the Joint Chiefs of Staff, assembled his colleagues to discuss options. He pushed Blue Spoon as the best course of action, but he wanted their input and consensus. He got it. Powell then conferred with the top advisors of President George Bush Sr., and secured their commitment as well.

In short, Powell touched all the bases. He followed written procedures, and he also observed all the relevant informal protocols. And yet, as he remembers:

> *The last night before the invasion,*
> *sitting alone in the dark in the back seat*
> *of my car on the drive home, I felt*
> *full of foreboding. I was going to be*
> *involved in conducting a war, one that*
> *I had urged, one that was sure to*
> *spill blood. Had I been right? Had my*
> *advice been sound?... What would*
> *our casualties be? How many civilians*
> *might lose their lives in the fighting?*

By the next day, Powell (at least outwardly) was calm and confident. But he had already been through his midnight moment of aloneness—that long moment of self-doubt, second-guessing, and deep anxiety that is reserved for leaders.

Throughout his career, Powell saw his own superiors—both military and civilian—struggling with the same kind of loneliness. Powell recounts a poignant episode in a darkened airplane when his then boss, the normally hard-edged Caspar Weinberger, made a rare display of emotion. Holding power, Weinberger told his young subordinate, is both lonely and exhausting. "You make real enemies but few real friends," Weinberger said. "It exhausts a man in body and spirit." From a seemingly unflappable leader—a man whose nickname during his stint at the head of the Office of Management and Budget was "Cap the Knife"—this was a surprising admission.

We need to remind ourselves, of course, that leaders *seek out* these responsibilities, and for the most part assume authority with their eyes open. They have accepted (and even asked for) those heavy weights on their shoulders. They revel in the exercise of the authority that comes along with those weights. And to some extent, they miss those weights when they are finally removed. As Powell half-jokingly used to tell audiences during his public speaking days: "One of the saddest figures in all Christendom is the chairman of the Joint Chiefs of Staff, once removed, driving around with a baseball cap pulled over his eyes, making his strategic choice as to whether it's going to be McDonald's or Taco Bell."

So, as Powell says, "Command is lonely." The prescription seems to be to assume command and its corollary—with your eyes wide open. You can expect that some very tough decisions will go along with the perks associated with high office, and you can expect to experience some periodic anxiety when your decisions may put lives or organizations in peril. So make sure that you're comfortable having the buck stop on your desk, well before it actually gets there.

· BUT "LONELY" IS NO EXCUSE

The final responsibility for the success or failure of a mission rests with the leader. I've proposed that real leaders *take* that responsibility, willingly and unquestionably. They don't make excuses after the fact, or scapegoat, or backpedal. Responsible leaders take ownership of setbacks and errors, and then constructively focus on analyzing the problem and fixing it.

Success has a thousand parents; failure is an orphan. In the wake of a management misstep, it is tempting for the organization's leaders to explain how a particular mistake has a broad base of ownership. This is partly ego, but there may also be some rationalization going on: *If we step up to the plate and own this mistake 100 percent, won't that undermine our authority?*

In fact, the opposite is true. Great leaders own the mistakes and let others own the victories—and their own stature is greatly enhanced by both actions. As we've seen, Powell's willingness to accept full responsibility for his decisions throughout his career not only has won him loyalty from his troops, but also has played a key role in his career ascent. People forgive mistakes that (1) are understandable and (2) are owned by their authors.

And this is greatly magnified by a demonstrated willingness to share the *triumphs* of leadership with others. After the Gulf War victory in 1991, the editors of *U.S. News & World Report* let Powell know that they intended to put his picture on the magazine's cover. To their surprise, Powell tried at length to convince them to put General Norman Schwarzkopf, the field commander of Desert Storm, on its cover instead. My guess is that had Desert Storm failed, and had *U.S. News* proposed putting Powell on its cover as the "guilty party," Powell would not have argued with that choice. He wouldn't have been happy, of course (who would?), but he would have accepted the responsibility as his own.

OFFSETTING LONELINESS

The initial heading for this section was "combating loneliness," but after reflection, I determined that that was the wrong message. Loneliness (and the prospect of loneliness, and the aftermath of loneliness) is an integral part of the leadership experience. Each such experience is a sort of purifying fire. It helps prepare the leader for the next crisis down the road. So the point is not to minimize loneliness, but instead to offset its counterproductive aspects.

One way of doing this is to make sure that *everything about your agenda is perfectly clear in advance*. This minimizes "he said/she said" kinds of recriminations, after the fact. I'm the leader. If I'm going to take responsibility for this decision, and the actions that grow out of my decision, then I want to make damn sure that the organization gets my message right before it implements. I want the organization to see me "owning" this decision in advance, in its entirety. I want complete clarity of detail, and of ownership.

It is said that in advance of a significant action, Napoleon would call in the person he considered to be his corporal. (A corporal was the lowest-ranking officer who had direct reports.) He would read his orders to the corporal, and ask him to interpret what he thought those orders meant. If the corporal's response was accurate, Napoleon knew that every other officer and noncommissioned officer in his army would understand the orders as well.

So loneliness can't—or shouldn't—be avoided, but it should be offset. Clear communication is a vital tool. In times of crisis, the leader must paint an absolutely clear picture of what needs to happen. In effect, the leader is painting the picture that he or she will own, after the fact. The process of creating that picture not only clarifies the leader's thinking, but also reinforces his or her stature as a leader. When the time comes to celebrate victory (or own up to defeat), the organization is far more likely to close ranks behind the leader.

SETTING THE ULTIMATE EXAMPLE

Serving as a role model is one of the most important functions of an effective leader. We've considered this lesson in previous chapters, but it's worth mentioning again in this context. "The leader sets an example," asserts Powell. "Whether in the Army or in civilian life, the other people in the organization take their cue from the leader—not from what the leader says, but what the leader does."

Everyone in the organization is a "boss watcher." The leader is always in a glass house, and that's a lonely position. People pay attention to what the boss says, and they pay even more attention to what he or she does. People carefully track what their boss pays attention to: what questions he asks, what reports she asks for and reads, what meeting agenda priorities he sets, what kinds of resources she allocates to which part of the enterprise, whom he criticizes and for what, what thrills or angers her, whom he lauds and for what, whom she promotes, whom he assigns to the lucrative project, whom she visits and hangs out with, and so on.

People observe these things, and then—regardless of the boss's words—they draw conclusions about what's *really* important. Based on his own experiences, Powell has often said that "setting an example" is the single most important role of the leader.

Leaders who set the example, or "model the way"—to use the phrase of my colleagues Jim Kouzes and Barry Posner—have the greatest credibility and influence with the people who work with them. But if there's a mismatch in the audio of the leader's talk and the video of his or her behavior, unit performance and morale plummet. As Powell observes,

> *You can issue all the memos and give all the motivational speeches you want, but if the rest of the people in your organization don't see you putting forth your best effort every single day, they won't either.*

The leader is the ultimate role model that everyone watches carefully, and that lonely position is one that many managers seem reticent to fill. For a leader, loudly calling out for a big change in the organization but then not visibly "living" that change is the height of folly. If an executive is stating that being customer-centric is now a corporate priority, but he himself is not spending a lot more time with customers, then he's not walking the talk. He's not doing the work of leadership. If she doesn't personally and publicly follow through to insure that performance metrics, sourcing, logistics, scheduling, information systems and compensation reflect a customer-centric priority, she's not walking the talk. She's not doing the work of leadership. And people know it. Which means it's far less likely that customer-centric work will be done by anybody.

The same criteria apply to more intangible factors like organizational values and norms. If a leader verbally espouses honesty, candor, open door communication, collaboration, or risk-taking, then that leader—more than anyone else!—must visibly support and demonstrate those virtues. When people are confident that they can *count on their leader*, they are more likely to demonstrate those virtues themselves. This brings up a further point. It's not merely that the leader himself must be honest, candid, and so on. The leader must also help insure that employees who do the same are properly acknowledged, rewarded—and when necessary, protected.

Ineffectual leaders act as if it is not their responsibility to set the primary example for a strategy, change effort, or value set. Good leaders recognize that setting the first and foremost example is not a function they can, or should delegate. By their own actions, they signify that setting the example is their obligation to those they lead.

Powell's maxim, "always do your best, because someone is watching" is one which he's used as career advice to upwardly mobile employees. As we now see, it's even more applicable to leaders themselves because whether they like it or not, someone—actually everyone—is watching closely. Good leaders willingly take on this often lonely role, knowing that by doing so they create an even better organization for the future.

THE FINAL STAGE OF LONELINESS

Powell has already introduced this topic for us. If leadership is lonely, then giving up leadership is lonely, as well. The image of the former chairman of the Joint Chiefs of Staff debating between McDonald's and Taco Bell is both funny and poignant.

Nevertheless, great leaders know when it's time to leave the stage. Perhaps they sense their value is diminishing and their influence waning. Or perhaps, as in the case of Powell in the twilight of his military career, it's simply that their interests move elsewhere and they decide it's time to give the organization the benefit of some new blood.

That's not to say it's easy. In the wake of his voluntary retirement from the military, Powell recalled how difficult that process occasionally was. He sometimes jokingly described how he had gone from being the commander of the world's most powerful armed forces one day to being a full-time husband who was expected to repair a broken garbage disposal unit the next day.

Nevertheless, the responsibility for a graceful and timely exit is part of the loneliness and nobility of command. Powell likes to quote Thomas Jefferson's eloquent and modest first inaugural address: "I advance with obedience to the work, ready to retire from it whenever you become sensible how much better choice it is in your power to make." But in fact, the good leader steps down well before the citizenry or the rank and file start to demand a change. The good leader prepares the ranks beneath him or her for the next phase of organizational life, and then moves on.

SUMMARY

Everyone in an organization is called upon to make sacrifices of one kind or another. But leaders are called upon to make sacrifices of a special sort. They must make decisions that put the enterprise at risk—most often, to save it from a peril at hand. They must live with the suspense that accompanies the arrival of the "verdict": Was it the right call or the wrong call? They must live with the aftermath of the decision, taking responsibility when things go badly, and sharing the credit when things go well.

Throughout, they also sacrifice themselves in order to serve as role models. They subject themselves to relentless scrutiny, perform at 100 percent, and serve as primary examples of the priorities, values, and behaviors they espouse. Then, when the time comes, they decide to give up their power and authority, and thereby make room for a new generation of leaders.

By now, of course, you've realized that the leadership secrets of Colin Powell are not really secrets at all. You've probably met them all in some other guise. They are the code of a deeply principled individual who has assumed positions of increasing responsibility over a long and distinguished career. They're all about some basic tasks of leadership: committing 100% to a shared mission, elevating performance standards, challenging the status quo, attending to details, surrounding oneself with talent, challenging experts, simplifying messages, empowering people in the field, selectively pissing people off, showing courage and resolve, having fun, and much more.

All of these principles are easy to comprehend, and all of them are damnably difficult to live and make happen. And that explains why truly great leaders are rare indeed.

So the community of great leaders is a small one. But I believe it's a community whose doors are open—open to those who are willing to work hard to meet the high standards described in this book. They are Powell's standards, but they are also the property of everyone who chooses to embrace them.

The last word is Colin Powell's. Typically, it gets right to the point:

"Leadership is not rank, privilege, titles, or money. It is responsibility."

That's a fitting finale to this chapter, to this book, and to the aspirations of anyone who wants to truly *earn* the title of leader.

POWELL PRINCIPLES

1. **Command is lonely**. The ultimate decision rests with the leader, and strong leaders accept the weight of their position.

2. **Lead by example.** All employees are boss watchers. The rank and file will always take their cues from the leader. It is therefore doubly important that the leader live the values he or she espouses.

3. **Know when to exit.** Just when you've figured it all out, it's time to pass it along to the next generation. Sometimes the act of leaving is the greatest task of leadership. Know when it's time.

4. **Leadership is, ultimately, responsibility, and, it's the ultimate responsibility.** Those who seek out responsibility have to be prepared to accept it, fully and unequivocally. Lead as though "the buck stops here."

Quotations From Chairman Powell:
A LEADERSHIP PRIMER
by Oren Harari

I HAVE LITTLE INTEREST in celebrities. If I were the rule rather than the exception, *Hard Copy* and *People* would go out of business fast. So, earlier this year, when General Colin Powell made the transformation from a human being to phenomenon, and when his nationwide book-signing tour became a happening to frenzied masses—well, I paid little attention. I didn't buy the book, either.

Then I found myself on the same speaking platform as Powell. Charitably speaking, I was the opening act in front of 1,000 bankers who were there to see the main show. I stuck around to see it, too, and frankly, I was impressed. Powell was witty, erudite, insightful, articulate and self-deprecating. All commendable virtues. So I decided to buy the book

Am I glad I did! *My American Journey* is a marvelous work, and it provided an unexpected payoff. As I read it, I started to underline noteworthy phrases and sentences and soon realized that what I was underlining were gems of wisdom regarding effective leadership. In fact, when I was finished, I was ready to toss out every leadership book in my library.

I'd like to share with you a compendium of advice from the general. With the exception of the occasional paraphrase to keep grammatical consistency (which will be noted), I present Powell's words verbatim in italics—18 priceless lessons, to be exact. After each quotation from General Powell, I attach my own civilian commentary, which I hope you will find useful.

LESSON ONE

Being responsible sometimes means pissing people off. Good leadership involves responsibility to the welfare of the group, which means that some people will get angry at your actions and decisions. It's inevitable—if you're honorable.

Trying to get everyone to like you is a sign of mediocrity. You'll avoid the tough decisions, you'll avoid confronting the people who need to be confronted, and you'll avoid offering differential rewards based on differential performance because some people might get upset. Ironically, by procrastinating on the difficult choices, by trying not to get anyone mad, and by treating everyone equally "nicely" regardless of their contributions, you'll simply ensure that the only people you'll wind up angering are the most creative and productive people in the organization.

LESSON TWO

The day soldiers stop bringing you their problems is the day you have stopped leading them. They have either lost confidence that you can help them or concluded that you do not care. Either case is a failure of leadership. If this were a litmus test, the majority of CEOs would fail. One, they build so many barriers to upward communication that the very idea of someone lower in the hierarchy looking up to the leader for help is ludicrous. Two, the corporate culture they foster often defines asking for help as weakness or failure, so people cover up their gaps, and the organization suffers accordingly: Real leaders make themselves accessible and available. They show concern for the efforts and challenges faced by underlings—even as they demand high standards. Accordingly, they are more likely to create an environment where problem analysis replaces blame.

LESSON THREE

Don't be buffaloed by experts and elites. Experts often possess more data than judgment. Elites can become so inbred that they produce hemophiliacs who bleed to death as soon as they are nicked by the real world! Small companies and startups don't have the time for analytically detached experts. They don't have the money to subsidize lofty elites, either. The president answers the phone and drives the truck when necessary; everyone on the payroll visibly produces and contributes to bottom-line results or they're history. But as companies get bigger; they often forget who "brung them to the dance": things like all-hands involvement, egalitarianism, informality, market intimacy, daring, risk, speed, agility. Policies that emanate from ivory towers often have an adverse impact on the people out in the field who are fighting the wars or bringing in the revenues. Real leaders are vigilant—and combative—in the face of these trends.

LESSON FOUR

Don't be afraid to challenge the pros, even in their own backyard. Learn from the pros, observe them, seek them out as mentors and partners. But remember that even the pros may have leveled out in terms of their learning and skills. Sometimes even the pros can become complacent and lazy. Leadership does not emerge from blind obedience to anyone. Xerox's Barry Rand was right on target when he warned his people that if you have a yes-man working for you, one of you is redundant. Good leadership encourages everyone's evolution.

LESSON FIVE

Never neglect details. When everyone's mind is dulled or distracted the leader must be doubly vigilant. Strategy equals execution. All the great ideas and visions in the world are worthless if they can't be implemented rapidly and efficiently. Good leaders delegate and empower others liberally, but they pay attention to details, every day. (Think about supreme athletic coaches like Jimmy Johnson, Pat Riley and Tony La Russa.) Bad ones—even those who fancy themselves as progressive "visionaries"—think they're somehow "above" operational details. Paradoxically, good leaders understand something else: An obsessive *routine* in carrying out the details begets conformity and complacency, which in turn dulls everyone's mind. That is why even as they pay attention to details, they continually encourage people to challenge the process. They implicitly understand the sentiment of CEO-leaders like Quad/Graphic's Harry Quadracci, Oticon's Lars Kolind and the late Bill McGowan of MCI, who all independently asserted that the job of a leader is not to be the chief organizer but the chief *dis*-organizer.

LESSON SIX

You don't know what you can get away with until you try. You know the expression "it's easier to get forgiveness than permission?" Well, it's true. Good leaders don't wait for official blessing to try things out. They're prudent, not reckless. But they also realize a fact of life in most organizations: If you ask enough people for permission, you'll inevitably come up against someone who believes his job is to say "no." So the moral is, don't ask. I'm serious. In my own research with colleague Linda Mukai, we found that less effective middle managers endorsed the sentiment, "If I haven't explicitly been told 'yes,' I can't do it," whereas the good ones believed "If I haven't explicitly been told 'no,' I can." There's a world of difference between these two points of view.

LESSON SEVEN

Keep looking below surface appearances. Don't shrink from doing so (just) because you might not like what you find. "If it ain't broke, don't fix it" is the slogan of the complacent, the arrogant or the scared. It's an excuse for inaction, a call to non-arms. It's a mind-set that assumes (or hopes) that today's realities will continue tomorrow in a tidy, linear and predictable fashion. Pure fantasy. In this sort of culture you won't find people who proactively take steps to solve problems as they emerge. Here's a little tip: Don't invest in these companies.

LESSON EIGHT

Organization doesn't really accomplish anything. Plans don't accomplish anything, either. Theories of management don't much matter. Endeavors succeed or fall because of the people involved. Only by attracting the best people will you accomplish great deeds. In a brain-based economy, your best assets are people. We've heard this expression so often that it's become trite. But how many leaders really "walk the talk" with this stuff? Too often, people are assumed to be empty chess pieces to be moved around by grand viziers, which may explain why so many top managers immerse their calendar time in deal-making, restructuring and the latest management fad. How many immerse themselves in the goal of creating an environment where the best, the brightest, the most creative are attracted, retained and—most importantly—unleashed?

LESSON NINE

Organization charts and fancy titles count for next to nothing. Organization charts are frozen, anachronistic photos in a workplace that ought to be as dynamic as the external environment around you. If people really followed organization charts, companies would collapse. In well-run organizations, titles are also pretty meaningless. At best, they advertise some authority—an official status conferring the ability to give orders and induce obedience. But titles mean little in terms of real power, which is the capacity to influence and inspire. Have you ever noticed that people will personally commit to certain individuals who on paper (or on the org chart) possess little authority—but instead possess pizzazz, drive, expertise and genuine caring for teammates and products? On the flip side, nonleaders in management may be formally anointed with all the perks and frills associated with high positions, but they have little influence on others, apart from their ability to extract minimal compliance to minimal standards.

LESSON TEN

Never let your ego get so close to your position that when your position goes, your ego goes with it. Too often, change is stifled by people who cling to familiar turfs and job descriptions. One reason that even large organizations wither is that managers won't challenge old, comfortable ways of doing things. But real leaders understand that, nowadays, every one of our jobs is becoming obsolete. The proper response is to obsolete our activities before someone else does. Effective leaders create a climate where people's worth is determined by their willingness to learn new skills and grab new responsibilities, thus perpetually reinventing their jobs. The most important question in performance evaluation becomes not. "How well did you perform your job since the last time we met?" but, "How much did you change it?"

LESSON ELEVEN

Fit no stereotypes. Don't chase the latest management fads. The situation dictates which approach best accomplishes the team's mission. Flitting from fad to fad creates team confusion, reduces the leader's credibility and drains organizational coffers. Blindly following a particular fad generates rigidity in thought and action. Sometimes speed to market is more important than total quality. Sometimes an unapologetic directive is more appropriate than participatory discussion. To quote Powell, some situations require the leader to hover closely; others require long, loose leashes. Leaders honor their core values, but they are flexible in how they execute them. They understand that management techniques are not magic mantras but simply tools to be reached for at the right times.

LESSON TWELVE

Perpetual optimism is a force multiplier. The ripple effect of a leader's enthusiasm and optimism is awesome. So is the impact of cynicism and pessimism. Leaders who whine and blame engender those same behaviors among their colleagues. I am not talking about stoically accepting organizational stupidity and performance incompetence with a "what, me worry?" smile. I am talking about a gung ho attitude that says "we can change things here, we can achieve awesome goals, we can be the best." Spare me the grim litany of the "realist"; give me the unrealistic aspirations of the optimist any day.

LESSON THIRTEEN

"Powell's Rules for Picking People"—Look for intelligence and judgment and, most critically, a capacity to anticipate, to see around corners. Also look for loyalty, integrity, a high energy drive, a balanced ego and the drive to get things done. How often do our recruitment and hiring processes tap into these attributes? More often than not, we ignore them in favor of length of resume, degrees and prior titles. A string of job descriptions a recruit held yesterday seem to be more important than who one is today, what she can contribute tomorrow or how well his values mesh with those of the organization. You can train a bright, willing novice in the fundamentals of your business fairly readily, but it's a lot harder to train someone to have integrity, judg-

ment, energy, balance and the drive to get things done. Good leaders stack the deck in their favor right in the recruitment phase.

LESSON FOURTEEN

(Borrowed by Powell from Michael Korda): Great leaders are almost always great simplifiers who can cut through argument, debate and doubt, to offer a solution everybody can understand! Effective leaders understand the KISS principle, or Keep It Simple, Stupid. They articulate vivid, overarching goals and values, which they use to drive daily behaviors and choices among competing alternatives. Their visions and priorities are lean and compelling, not cluttered and buzzword-laden. Their decisions are crisp and clear, not tentative and ambiguous. They convey an unwavering firmness and consistency in their actions, aligned with the picture of the future they paint. The result? Clarity of purpose, credibility of leadership, and integrity in organization.

LESSON FIFTEEN

Part 1: Use the formula P=40 to 70, in which P stands for the probability of success and the numbers indicate the percentage of information acquired. Part II: Once the information is in the 40 to 70 range, go with your gut. Powell's advice is don't take action if you have only enough information to give you less than a 40 percent

chance of being right, but don't wait until you have enough facts to be 100 percent sure, because by then it is almost always too late. His instinct is right: Today, excessive delays in the name of information-gathering breeds "analysis paralysis." Procrastination in the name of reducing risk actually increases risk

LESSON SIXTEEN

The commander in the field is always right and the rear echelon is wrong, unless proved otherwise. Too often, the reverse defines corporate culture. This is one of the main reasons why leaders like Ken Iverson of Nucor Steel, Percy Barnevik of Asea Brown Boveri, and Richard Branson of Virgin have kept their corporate staffs to a bare-bones minimum. (And I do mean minimum— how about fewer than 100 central corporate staffers for global $30 billion-plus ABB? Or around 25 and 3 for multi-billion Nucor and Virgin, respectively?) Shift the power and the financial accountability to the folks who are bringing in the beans, not the ones who are counting or analyzing them.

LESSON SEVENTEEN

Have fun in your command. Don't always run at a breakneck pace. Take leave when you've earned it. Spend time with your families. Corollary: Surround yourself with people who take their work seriously, but not themselves, those who work hard and play hard!

Herb Kelleher of Southwest Air and Anita Roddick of The Body Shop would agree: Seek people who have some balance in their lives, who are fun to hang out with, who like to laugh (at themselves, too) and who have some non-job priorities which they approach with the same passion that they do their work. Spare me the grim workaholic or the pompous pretentious "professional;" I'll help them find jobs with my competitor.

LESSON EIGHTEEN

Command is lonely. Harry Truman was right. Whether you're a CEO or the temporary head of a project team, the buck stops here. You can encourage participative management and bottom-up employee involvement, but ultimately, the essence of leadership is the willingness to make the tough, unambiguous choices that will have an impact on the fate of the organization. I've seen too many nonleaders flinch from this responsibility. Even as you create an informal, open, collaborative corporate culture, prepare to be lonely.

Well, there it is—a primer worthy of perusal by any aspiring leader and one a lot more useful than the infamous *Quotations* from Chairman Mao. I hope these lessons provide you the same road to success that they provided General Powell. Good luck!

This article is reprinted from the December 1996 issue of the American Management Association magazine *Management Review*, © 1996 by Oren Harari.

Sources/Notes

IN RESEARCHING THIS book, hundreds of sources—articles, books, Web sites, speeches, government reports, etc.—were accessed and then narrowed down to those cited here. Colin Powell, though in no way involved with any aspect of the writing of this book, provided me with several original documents and personal notes which proved invaluable in providing insight into his leadership style and philosophy. He also pointed me in the right direction in locating other published sources that were very useful.

Among the many secondary sources that provided rich insights into Powell's history and philosophy (all are cited below), his superb autobiography *My American Journey* (Random House, 1995) deserves special mention. While I often augmented them with material from other sources, several salient insights and anecdotes came from this book, including the following:

Powell's reassessment of the post-Cold War military needs, his experiences in Iran and Vietnam, his pivotal role in the Gulf War, his personal thoughts on the so-called "Powell Doctrine," and his relationships with luminaries such as Mikhael Gorbachev, Dick Cheney, and George Bush Sr.

In researching Colin Powell, it became apparent that several of the quotes/stories have been "published" in multiple places. An Internet search of a particular topic would often yield multiple results, including my own "Colin Powell Primer," ("Quotations from Chairman Powell: A Leadership Primer," *Management Review*, December 1996), which appears in the appendix that precedes this section. When the original provenance of a particular quote or story could be established, I have sourced it below.

PROLOGUE
"Leadership is the art of accomplishing more..." Colin Powell with Joseph E. Persico, *My American Journey* (New York: Random House, 1995), p. 258.

CHAPTER 1
"Making people mad was part of being a leader..." *My American Journey*, p. 321.

"...more than half the companies that appeared on the 1980 *Fortune* 500..." Price Pritchett & Associates "New Work Habits For A Radically Changing World."

"I'll be frank. From time to time..." *My American Journey*.

"I'll bet you right now that there's no established organization..." "Follow the Leader" *Context Magazine* Feb/March 2000.

" There are times when leaders have to act..." Donald Rumsfeld's Confirmation Hearing, http://www.staugustine.com/stories/011701/nat_0117010045.shtml.

"If you perform well, we'll get along fine..." "Town Hall Meeting" speech, Jan. 25, 2001, Washington, D.C. From the U.S. Department of State web site, www.state.gov/secretary/index.cfm?docid=24&CFNoCache=TRUE&printfriendly=true, visited Oct. 17, 2001

CHAPTER 2

"What will make things different in the 21st century..." Anonymous, "Colin Powell's Thoughts on Leadership," *Industry Week*, Aug 19, 1996.

"We beat them on the field of ideas..." "Town Hall Meeting" speech.

" You will find an open style..." Ibid.

"When a captain came in to see me..." "Follow the Leader" *Context Magazine*.

"I also knew that, when he got back to his office..." Ibid.

"In the military, when you become a four-star general..." Ibid.

"He jumps over layers of bureaucracy..." Kevin Whitelaw and Stefan Lovgren, "Colin Powell's way. His style wins praise, but the big policy fights still lie ahead; South Africa," *U.S. News & World Report* Jun 4, 2001.

"With the end of the Cold War came the explosion..." "Town Hall Meeting" speech.

"I'm looking for leaders in public diplomacy..." Ibid.

"They would tell me when I did something..." "Follow the Leader" *Context Magazine*.

"Money is a coward..." DeWayne Wickham, "Powell trip wins points for Bush," *USA Today* 08/13/2001.

CHAPTER 3

"In the military, to put it in corporate terms..." Gerry Romano, "Never Walk Past a Mistake," *Association Management*, October 1998.

"I saw it as my main mission..." *My American Journey* p. 436.

"...it's not clear whether the new money will go toward truly changing..." Greg Jaffe and Anne Marie Squeo, "Moving Targets: As Money Pours In, Will the Military Get The Right Arsenal?" *Wall Street Journal* Sep 19, 2001.

"First, you need to understand that Russia is not coming back..." www.issues2000.org/Colin_Powell_Foreign_Policy.htm

"We will need to work together well..." Colin Powell, "Confirmation Hearing" speech, Jan. 17, 2001, Washington, D.C. From the U.S. Department of State web site, http://www.state.gov/s/h/tst/index.cfm?docid=443, visited Oct. 17, 2001.

"This world is changing so much..." Colin Powell, remarks at the Roundtable Meeting of the Leaders of the Campaign to Preserve U.S. Global Leadership, July 10, 2001, Washington, D.C. Distributed by the Office of International Information Programs, U.S. Department of State; web site http://usinfo.state.gov.

"It's the little things that have State Department workers cooing..." Paul Bedard, Chitra Ragavan, and Kevin Whitelaw, "Man For All Seasons," *U.S. News & World Report* May 21, 2001.

CHAPTER 4

"You pay the king his shilling..." *My American Journey* p. 321.

"Generate the interest of 'the led'..." "Colin Powell's Thoughts on Leadership," *Industry Week*.

" Hey, I personally don't care if you hold reveille..." *My American Journey* p. 320.

"If you screw up, just vow to do better..." Ibid. p. 321.

"Freedom to be your best means nothing..." Jan Hemming, Interview with General Colin Powell *Priorities*.

"Supplicants don't get respect..." Anna Muoio, "Women and Men, Work and Power," *Fast Company* Issue 13, page 71.

CHAPTER 5

Story about Iran and the overthrow of the Shah's regime is from *My American Journey* p. 242.

"It is best to get the facts out..." *My American Journey* p. 282

"Untidy truth is better than smooth lies..." Ibid. p. 285.

"I have not allowed myself to be coerced..." Lisa Shaw, ed., *In His Own Words: Colin Powell* (New York: The Berkeley Publishing Group, 1995), p. 93.

CHAPTER 6

"This particular emperor expects to be told..." *My American Journey* p. 320.

"The key decision that came out of that meeting is..." Frontline Interview Transcript, *Public Broadcasting System,* http://www.pbs.org/wgbh/pages/frontline/gulf/oral/powell/1.html.

"...to draw a line in the sand now..." Ibid.

"Perhaps I was the ghost of Vietnam..." Ibid.

"...if military action widens..." "A General Who Paints," *The Economist* Oct 20, 2001.

"On an organizational level, the still murky war..." Michael Hirsh and Roy Gutman, "Powell in the Middle," *Newsweek* Oct 1, 2001.

"The President seems to be in Powell's corner..." Ibid.

"I always find it much better to try to solve problems..." Johanna McGeary, "Odd Man Out," *Time* Sept. 10, 2001.

CHAPTER 7

"...we had entered into a halfhearted half-war..." *My American Journey* p. 148.

"...were fine if beneath them lay a solid mission..." Ibid. p. 291.

"We take down Noriega, we take the whole Panamanian..." Frontline Interview Transcript, *Public Broadcasting System,* http://www.pbs.org/wgbh/pages/frontline/gulf/oral/powell/1.html.

"You do not squander courage and lives..." *My American Journey* p. 148.

"No one starts a war, or rather no one in his senses should do so…" Carl von Clausewitz, *On War*, trans. Michael Howard and Peter Paret (Princeton, N.J.: Princeton University Press, 1989), p. 579.

"As soon as they tell me…" Michael R Gordon, "Powell Delivers a Resounding No on Using Limited Force in Bosnia," *New York Times* Sep 28, 1992 Start Page: A1.

"It will not be over…" "State Department Press Briefing," Sep 17, 2001.

"[Once] we have looked at all the rough edges…" "Town Hall Meeting" speech.

"I had fought the good fight…" *My American Journey* p. 221.

"I expect you to convey upward to me…" "Town Hall Meeting" speech.

CHAPTER 8
"I don't know that leadership in the 21st century…" "Colin Powell's thoughts on leadership," *Industry Week*.

"…the most important assets you have in all of this are the people…" Gerry Romano, "Never walk past a mistake," *Association Management* Oct 1998.

"Officers have been trying for hundreds of years…" *My American Journey* p. 216.

"Our ability to successfully perform our mission depends…" "Remarks at the Department of State Awards Ceremony," May 10, 2001, Washington, D.C. From the U.S. Department of State web site, www.state.gov, visited Oct. 17, 2001.

"I also believe, to the depth of my heart…" "Town Hall Meeting" speech.

"We've got to spend wisely and well…" *My American Journey* p. 403.

"If you don't fire people who are not doing the job…" "Follow the Leader," *Context Magazine*.

"The day I was promoted to three stars…" Ibid.

"He expected me to retire…" Ibid.

"You give me the right people…" Ibid.

"It takes a new team a few months to get acquainted…" Brian Friel, "The Powell Leadership Doctrine," http://www.govexec.com/features/0601/0601s1.htm June 1, 2001.

"I am going to fight for you…" "Town Hall Meeting" speech.

"At the end of the day, it's some soldier…" "Follow the Leader," *Context Magazine*.

CHAPTER 9
"…a general's attention to detail lets the soldier…" *My American Journey* p. 446.

"I have an insatiable demand to be in charge of the information…" *In His Own Words: Colin Powell* p. 93.

"If you are going to achieve excellence in big things…" *My American Journey* p. 198.

"Those of you who are leaders…" "Town Hall Meeting" speech.

"When everyone's mind is dulled or distracted…" *My American Journey* p. 109.

"We must be involved according to our national interests…" Colin Powell, "Confirmation Hearing" speech.

"…had an insatiable curiosity for details…" Harriet Rubin, "Past Track to the Future," *Fast Company* Issue 46, page 167.

CHAPTER 10

"Vogue phrases such as 'power down'..." *My American Journey* pp. 319–320.

"I've seen many management situations where people just pretended..." "Never walk past a mistake." *Association Management.*

"It used to be that we had a unifying theory of the world..." Interview with Rebecca Spires, of the Sandia National Laboratories in Albuquerque, New Mexico, June 9, 2000.

CHAPTER 11

"When we are debating an issue..." *My American Journey* p. 320.

"It was a very tough time..." Howard Means, *Colin Powell, A Biography* (New York: Ballantine Books, 1992) p. 227.

"Management is a science, leadership is an art..." "Town Hall Meeting" speech.

"A good leader surrounds himself with people..." Curt Schleier, appears in *Investor's Business Daily* and http://www.leadershipdynamics.org/2000/6-19-00.htm.

CHAPTER 12

"The core of the clearance problem..." Thomas E. Ricks, "Air Force Officers Seethe Over the Ones that Got Away," *Washington Post.*

"Those of us back here exist not only to support the President..." "Town Hall Meeting" speech.

"You are right, and those of us back here..." Ibid.

"One of your greatest challenges in the Pentagon..." *Colin Powell, A Biography* p. 227.

CHAPTER 13

"Management is easy. Leadership is motivating..." "Town Hall Meeting" speech.

"The leader sets an example. Whether in the Army or..." "Interview with General Colin Powell," *Priorities.*

"Here's a leadership lesson I've learned..." "Never Walk Past a Mistake," *Association Management.*

"...integrity of the senior leadership..." *My American Journey* p. 155.

"It is more important to do what is right..." Curt Schleier article, *Investor's Business Daily.*

"If the troops are cold, you're cold..." "Colin Powell's thoughts on leadership," *Industry Week.*

"Here's a leadership lesson that I've learned..." "Never Walk Past a Mistake," *Association Management.*

CHAPTER 14

"his upbeat personality was refreshing..." George Shultz, *Turmoil and Triumph* (New York: Scribner's, 1993) p. 1005.

"Optimism has little to do with external reality..." Carla Cantor, "Studying the Dark Side's Sunny Alter Ego: Positive Psychology," from the *CBS Healthwatch* web site: http://cbshealthwatch.medscape.com/cx/viewarticle/226763_print.

"Pessimists have a way of permeating the atmosphere..." Carol Orsag Madigan, "Removing the Skeptic's Hat," *Controller Magazine* August 1998, p. 50.

"Our philosophy is that you only get back what you expect..." Colin Powell, quoted in "Achieving Balance in Law Enforcement Training Philosophy," *Tuebor*, vol. 6, no. 1, winter 2000.

Research suggesting optimistic presidential candidates win elections comes from Martin E. Seligman's book, *Learned Optimism : How to Change Your Mind & Your Life*.

CHAPTER 15

"I am 63 going on 64..." "Town Hall Meeting" speech.

"Do your work, and then go home..." Ibid.

"As a leader, you need to recognize that people need balance..." Dennis Volpe, "Civilian asks 'What is leadership?'" from web site: http://www.afmc.wpafb.af.mil/HQ-AFMC/PA/news/archive/2001/mar/Hanscom_civilianleadership.htm.

CHAPTER 16

"The last night before the invasion, sitting alone..." *My American Journey* p. 427.

"You make real enemies but few real friends..." Ibid. pp. 314-315.

"One of the saddest figures in all Christendom..." John F. Stacks, "The Powell Factor," *Time* July 10, 1995.

"The leader sets an example..." "Interview with General Colin Powell," *Priorities*.

"You can issue all the memos..." Ibid.

"Never, ever cut them (your crew) off and let them die..." "Civilian asks 'What is leadership?'" from web site: http://www.afmc.wpafb.af.mil/HQ-AFMC/PA/news/archive/2001/mar/Hanscom_civilianleadership.htm.

"Leadership is not rank, privilege, titles..." from Rotary Newsletter web site: http://www.rotary5020.org/newsletter/May_01.pdf.

Index